THE IDEA OF CAPITALISM BEFORE THE INDUSTRIAL REVOLUTION

Critical Issues in History

Series Editor: Donald T. Critchlow

THE IDEA OF CAPITALISM BEFORE THE INDUSTRIAL REVOLUTION

RICHARD GRASSBY

ROWMAN & LITTLEFIELD PUBLISHERS, INC.
Lanham • Boulder • New York • Oxford

ROWMAN & LITTLEFIELD PUBLISHERS, INC.

Published in the United States of America
by Rowman & Littlefield Publishers, Inc.
4720 Boston Way, Lanham, Maryland 20706
http://www.rowmanlittlefield.com

12 Hid's Copse Road
Cumnor Hill, Oxford OX2 9JJ, England

British Library Cataloguing in Publication Information Available

Library of Congress Cataloging-in-Publication Data

Grassby, Richard.
    The idea of capitalism before the Industrial Revolution / Richard
Grassby.
        p. cm. — (Critical issues in history)
    Includes bibliographical references and index.
    ISBN 0-8476-9632-4 (cloth : alk. paper). — ISBN 0-8476-9633-2
(paper : alk. paper)
        1. Capitalism. 2. Industrial revolution. 3. Economic history.
I. Title. II. Series.
HB501.G642 1999
330.12'2—dc21   99-34932
                                                            CIP

Printed in the United States of America

∞™ The paper used in this publication meets the minimum
requirements of American National Standard for Information
Sciences—Permanence of Paper for Printed Library Materials,
ANSI/NISO Z39.48–1992.

CONTENTS

SERIES EDITOR'S FOREWORD

The nature of capitalism and of free-market economies, as Richard Grassby explains, presents the student of economic history with a complex set of problems: What is the definition of capitalism? Are free-market economies the same as capitalist economies? What is the significance of capitalism to our understanding of economic development, social and political order, and culture? Indeed, when did capitalism first emerge? Finally, is capitalism good or bad?

In this book, Professor Grassby, a historian of seventeenth-century England, answers these questions by framing capitalism as a historical process that has changed over time. In providing this context for our understanding of capitalism, he posits that the idea of capitalism has symbolic importance but little historical reality or explanatory power when applied categorically to every economy, society, political regime, or culture. As a consequence, the significance of the idea of capitalism is that it is a creature of myth rather than historical reality. The development of economies, including market economies, is not predetermined but is conditioned by human action and the balance of power. Economic change occurs continuously and proceeds at an uneven pace. This change is not universal or absolute and therefore needs to be studied within the particularities and relative context of each society and historical period.

In stating his case that capitalism needs to be explained within specific historical contexts, Grassby reexamines the rich historical debate over the meaning of capitalism, the nature of production and exchange, the nature of contract, and the "spirit" of capitalism and its ideological rise in the industrial period. He offers to the reader a general definition of capitalism in terms of the market economy and the growth of financial markets and consumerism, but he qualifies this definition by arguing that these attributes must be located historically within each society. Moreover, he warns that many of the characteristics attributed to capitalism, including the concept of "modernity," were a consequence of the Industrial Revolution, which transformed the economic basis of society with its new technological and energy sources. Social scientists and historians, he adds, have focused their greatest attention on the transition from feudalism to capitalism, not on the transition to industrialism.

Readers of this terse study will find Grassby's work challenging and controversial. By arguing that capitalist development is an uneven historical process, without determined attributes or consequences, he challenges marxist, neoclassic, feminist, monetarist, rational-choice, and institutionalist theorists who have imposed deterministic, abstract models on historical developments unique to each given society. He accuses these theorists, both marxists and nonmarxists, of assuming the existence of the capitalist system and then looking to the historical record for illustrative examples. Instead, he calls for students of capitalism to grapple with the diverse and contradictory sources found in the historical record. Societies, he concludes, develop piecemeal and can continue to function even when certain sectors of the economic, political, and cultural sectors no longer function properly. Outcomes are not predetermined.

In the end, Grassby finds that central to understanding economic and social development is the importance of individual agency. Because societies are composed of individuals whose behavior cannot be predicted, all social systems are potentially unstable. Even capitalism with its great benefits (and costs) appears to have its own life cycle, falling victim to old age, lack of direction, disagreement over priorities, and incompatible ends. Yet neither its rise nor collapse can be determined. The task of the student of history is to examine the process of uneven and nonlinear development within specific localities by keeping in mind the importance of societal peculiarities and individual action. Perhaps one of the ironies of this conclusion is that Grassby agrees in the end with Karl Marx's observation that humankind makes its own history.

Donald T. Critchlow
Series Editor

1

WHAT IS CAPITALISM?

There are few characteristics of the modern world that have not been attributed to or blamed on capitalism. It is a concept invoked indiscriminately by everyone, from neomarxists to neoconservatives, from literary critics to political scientists and feminists, as an explanation for innovations in every field of human activity—economic, social, and cultural. Few have been able to agree, however, on what the term actually means. Within and between each school of thought, the debate, often in unintelligible jargon, over what constitutes the essence and significance of capitalism has been continuous and intractable. As early as 1918, Richard Passow listed 111 definitions of the term. Little consensus exists as to when capitalism first appeared, what form it assumed, or how it may have changed over time.

Capitalism is a system of ideas that owes little to the theoretical and ahistorical constructs of classical and neoclassical economics. Although it can function as a model of the relationships between different factors in an economy, it has been used primarily by socialists, sociologists, and historians and not by economists. When the term is featured in the works of John Maynard Keynes or Milton Friedman, it serves as a polemical label rather than as an analytical tool.

The idea of capitalism, like the notion of a world-system, is a composite or ideal type. Ideal types are neither theoretical postulates nor empirical categories, but fictive generalizations about the predominant characteristics of a particular society, projected from selected historical facts and intended to serve as a basis for universal analysis. The German sociologist Max Weber, for example, constructed the nature of capitalism from actual historical experience, concentrating on mentalities and on what the action of individuals and social groups would be if directed rationally to a given end. His ideal type was neither literal nor completely abstract, neither a hypothesis to be verified nor a general concept, but what capitalism would be under ideal conditions.

Weber's contemporary, the historian Werner Sombart, employed a similar but less precise ideal type. Sombart invented and was the first to popularize the idea of capitalism as both a historically constructed actuality and a conceptualized ideal. Karl Marx, in contrast, believed that history was an aid to understanding capitalism (an expression that he never used, but that can be equated with his "economic system"); however, the scientific laws of history had to be deduced by theorizing. In marxism, the capitalist system develops not in response to external stimulus but through its own inner logic.

Although manifested in history, capitalism is fundamentally a theoretical concept defined largely in terms of its opposite, socialism, with no physical reality or empirical base. It is best treated as a metaphor, like the Industrial Revolution or feudalism, both vague and amorphous terms invented long after the events that they purport to describe. What is essentially a passive model has, however, acquired a personality and life of its own and is frequently regarded as a real force with the capacity to effect change. Capitalism is credited with a sense of the future and has even been accorded emotions and a sense of irony.

ECONOMIC CONSTRUCTS

Capitalism is most commonly identified with the free enterprise system as distinct from both a traditional, collective economy and the modern, centrally administered, command economy of socialism. In everyday usage, the term *capitalism* has become a synonym for the market economy, which in its theoretically perfect form is autonomous and self-regulating. Supply and demand under conditions of free competition determine the price and quantity of goods and labor. Opportunity and risk regulate the level of investment. Resources are not allocated by gift exchange or through social and political institutions, but by impersonal exchange between buyers and sellers seeking to maximize their utility. The market, which can function in principle without any physical site, converts inputs into outputs, clears prices, and extends itself though integration of different sectors and functions. The market mechanism alleviates scarcity and, subject to constraints of time and information, satisfies the maximum possible selfish choices of the sovereign consumer at least cost. In contrast to a self-sufficient household economy, all production is geared to the market; distribution is in the hands of middlemen who buy both raw materials and finished goods for resale. The market defines status, creates obligations, distributes surpluses, promotes specialization of function, and systematizes value.

Market capitalism of this kind has been postulated as the dynamic force in the early modern European economy since the publication of Adam Smith's *Wealth of Nations*. To Smith, the founder of Classical Economics, the division of labor, both within and between economies, increased efficiency and productivity, improved the quality of production, and lowered costs. To the historical geographer Fernand Braudel, the mobility of capital has been able to conquer both time and distance. He is, however, idiosyncratic in that he distinguishes between the market economy and capitalism. In his hierarchy of three economic systems, which coexist but do not overlap, the bottom level is perceived as an unchanging, cyclical, self-sufficient barter economy and the middle level as a simple exchange economy. Capitalism before the Industrial Revolution is then identified with a world economy of complex commodity and financial markets dominated by a succession of great cities—Venice, Antwerp, Genoa, Amsterdam, and London.

The American sociologist Immanuel Wallerstein has postulated a similar concept of a world economy stratified into zones. But his world-system, although it transcends national economies, is based on nation-states rather than on cities. Although early world economies, like that of Venice, are classified in his theory as precapitalist, he argues that a capitalist world economy emerged between 1450 and 1640 in the wake of geographical expansion and colonial settlement by Europeans, though some areas of the world were not incorporated until later. The windfall profits of the new markets and the import and circulation of American bullion created the necessary surplus of capital for investment. A tripartite geographical division of labor, linked by international trade, was established between a number of core states (with different political systems) and a dependent periphery and semi-periphery of primary producers.

As a neomarxist, Wallerstein argues that the world economy was based on the capitalist mode of production and on class differentiation; the surplus production of the periphery drains to the core. But his theory of core and periphery, each with a different mode of labor and type of production, allows feudalism to coexist with capitalism. Whereas in traditional marxist theory, free labor is a prerequisite of capitalism, Wallerstein treats the coerced labor of slaves as a capitalist institution and envisages a world economy supplied by seigneurial production. In contrast to earlier marxists, Wallerstein demotes the importance of wage labor and emphasizes external market forces rather than internal production factors.

Other theorists have focused on capital investment rather than on the market. A capitalist economy is defined simply as one in which capital predominates and is invested in production rather than in consumption. This presupposes a money economy with a standard measure of value (in contrast to a natural or subsistence economy) and a sufficient surplus to cover current needs while exchanging that surplus. The direction and timing of investment is determined by relative yield and by the cost/benefit ratio. An economy is regarded as capitalist when it has a high ratio of fixed to circulating capital and a high capital/output ratio with an increasing proportion of capital goods. The essence of capitalism is defined as continuous reinvestment; the standard of measurement becomes the ratio of net investment to Gross National Product.

A capital-intensive economy presupposes a high rate of saving and a rapid rate of aggregate capital formation. Investment capital can be accumulated from income and profits or by expropriation. Marx thought that primitive accumulation was achieved by extracting surplus labor value from the peasantry through ground rents and that the more efficient capitalists accumulated at the expense of their weaker competitors. Later marxists have emphasized the windfall profits of colonial expansion, especially the profit inflation supposedly generated by the influx of American silver. But investment capital can also be borrowed and some theorists have identified capitalism with the growth of private and public credit. The American economist, Joseph Schumpeter, although somewhat vague when he came to define capitalism, identified it with the private ownership of capital, profit making, and credit creation that disturbs the normal circular flow of the economy; he regarded the financial world as the command center.

Marx, on the other hand, focused not on the relations of exchange or on investment, but on the relations of production—that is, the social structure that was necessarily created by commodity production undertaken for profit. Marx defined capitalism as a mode of production. Exchange value only became dominant after productive relations had been alienated. Once the means of production had been appropriated and were owned by those with capital, those without capital had only their labor to sell. Labor became a commodity for hire and the workforce became a proletariat of wage contractors.

In marxist theory, social relations distinguish capitalist from pre-capitalist societies. Feudalism is regarded as a system of coerced labor; capitalism requires the abolition of serfdom and the monetarization of all obligations in a free labor market. Some differences exist between marxists as to the respective modes of production in the ancient world and in feudal Europe; one view is that two separate modes merged in the Renaissance. But orthodox marxists still argue that under feudalism production was for use or geared to local markets. They do not regard wealth as capital until it controls the means of production. Merchant capital is classified as precapitalist and subordinate to feudal overlords even after the growth of long-distance trade and the rise of the fiscal state.

SOCIAL AND POLITICAL STRUCTURE

Capitalism has also been equated with a particular system of social stratification. It is assumed that a market economy will create a market society in which roles are not ascribed by birth, that those with the best qualifications will be automatically selected. To liberal theorists, the new social order created by capitalism is hierarchical, but open, finely graduated, mobile, and meritocratic.

Other sociologists have, however, theorized that capitalism increased social tension, that greater inequality in the distribution of wealth and a more differentiated social system created role or class conflict. The French sociologist Emile Durkheim emphasized the loss of self-sufficiency and solidarity that resulted from the division of labor. By eliminating household production, Marx argued, capitalism depersonalized and alienated the workforce. The occupational status of the independent, self-employed craftsmen, who owned their tools and shop, was depressed and the wage laborers who replaced them were divorced from the means of production. In marxist theory, capitalism polarizes wealth and creates new antagonistic classes; civil society is dominated by the bourgeoisie who enjoy both economic and political power while peasants and artisans are reduced to a proletariat.

At the same time, capitalism has been identified with a broader change in the structure of society from gemeinschaft (community) to gesellschaft (association), in the classic terminology of the German sociologist Ferdnand Tonnies. In this model, precapitalist societies are defined as totally integrated, immobile, homogeneous, organic communities based on custom, reciprocity, status, and kinship, on a social rather than an economic division of labor, with no distinction between the individual and the social. These are superseded under capitalism by an impersonal market society, based on individualism, heterogeneity, contract, and private property rights. Customary obligations acquire a cash value and the fabric of community life is destroyed. Social transfers are replaced by individual exchange without regard for social costs. Market capitalism, based on individual self-interest and efficiency, defeats the moral economy, which is concerned with equity and communal values. Honor triumphs over interest, wants triumph over needs, and the market triumphs over society.

Since urbanization is virtually synonymous with civilization and with the market, capitalism has long been associated with towns rather than with the countryside. The high population density and the social fluidity of cities is thought by some to have favored the division of labor and economic individualism; urban contacts, it is argued, are secondary, segmental, and utilitarian. Urban populations and land use have been analyzed in marxist terms by historical geographers. According to location theory, towns with water communications are more likely to have distant markets and be market-oriented than landlocked towns, which are more authoritarian and less capitalist.

But most urban theories emphasize the administrative, ritualistic, and political roles of cities rather than their capitalistic function. Neomarxists have embraced the notion of agrarian capitalism and have dethroned the urban bourgeoisie. Central place theory argues that institutions and occupations that do not require space concentrate in cities and create new demand for goods, but the spatial relations between cities are interpreted more in social and cultural than in economic terms.

Capitalism has also been equated with the nuclear conjugal family and with the decline of traditional, group-based kinship. It is argued that the divorce of capital from labor eliminates household production and reduces the family to a unit of reproduction and consumption. The household becomes a domestic retreat, separate from the workplace, in which autonomous individuals with absolute property rights jealously guard the privacy of their separate spheres against community-based interference. The system of lineage and kinship, which in the past had provided some measure of social control in the absence of effective government, is destroyed because it is incompatible with a capitalist society. Weber thought that capitalism could only develop after business had been divorced from the household. In marxist theory, the survival of kinship and bureaucratic centralization obstructed the growth of a bourgeoisie and capitalism in Asia.

A similar theory holds that the introduction of individual private property rights transformed personal relations. Both the notion of romantic love and the exercise of free choice in marriage are attributed to capitalism. To Weber, romantic love was a cultural oddity (the opposite of rational, controlled capitalism); yet it served as an antidote to capitalist alienation and was necessary for the perpetuation and mental stability of an individualist society. An increase in illegitimacy has been linked to the emergence of wage labor; the growth of commodity production has been hypothetically linked with enhanced sexual freedom.

Theories of gender relations also connect capitalism with patriarchy. Friedrich Engels argued that the subjugation of women was a consequence of the introduction of private property, that the capitalist mode of production isolated women from the process of production and made them economically and emotionally dependent on their husbands and fathers. Capitalism divided wives into either idle bourgeois or proletarians. Feminist theorists, defining patriarchy broadly in physical, emotional, and spiritual terms, have differed on the questions of whether or not patriarchy preceded capitalism and how women were affected by the emergence of contract as an organizing principle. In capitalist society, some have argued, women are identified with and attacked as symbols of capital accumulation.

Capitalism has also been defined in terms of institutions rather than the market. Both at the micro level of the business firm and the macro level of the whole economy, emphasis is placed more on collective norms of behavior than on unbounded rationality. Business decisions are thought to depend on the internal power structure within firms as well as on prices in the market. Douglas North has constructed a theoretical model of economic development around a historical trend from high to low transaction costs; institutions create the incentive to channel effort into activities that bring the private rate of return close to the social rate of return.

To institutional theorists, the capitalist system rests on contract law and on an unabridged right to hold, assign, and exchange all types of private property. Contract is a cost-minimizing method of generating information about several opportunity choices for scarce resources. An autonomous market presupposes peace, a legal mechanism other than oaths to enforce bargains, private control of the means of production, free circulation of goods and labor, and the legal right both to exclude others and to alienate property. Owners must decide how assets should be employed, because they bear any losses incurred in the search for higher value from use. A capitalist society views all rights as property rights and rejects communal ownership, though the term *state capitalism* (a seeming contradiction in terms) is sometimes used to describe market-style economies in which the majority of fixed assets are owned and invested by the state, either directly or indirectly.

Capitalism has also been equated with specific business institutions such as the joint-stock company, with financial instruments such as the bank note, and with managerial techniques such as accountancy. The joint-stock company can indeed be regarded as the ancestor of the modern corporation; it both spread investment and risk among many shareholders and separated ownership from management. Sombart singled out double-entry bookkeeping (in which all transactions are recorded as a credit to one account and a debit to another) as the hallmark of early capitalism. Accountancy had to assume an objective economic reality that could be abstracted, classified, and measured; the move from narration to tabulation, as accounting developed, depersonalized the economic process.

Finally, capitalism is identified with the transition from a "domain" to a "tax" state, from household to national government. So long as government was patrimonial, there could be no clear distinction between public and private or between the state and society. Weber thought that the institutional structure of capitalism was created by the universal legal system of the bureaucratic state.

A capitalist economy cannot function without a unified, secure market and this requires a centralized polity that can maintain order, support a sound currency and fiscal policy, and codify and enforce the law. Even an uncompromising liberal like Friedrich Hayek recognized that the market needed rules and that states supplied necessary services. Others have argued that capitalist societies are ruled by politics and not by the market.

Some marxists have emphasized state formation as essential to capitalism. The political upheavals of the seventeenth century have been represented as a failure to overcome obstacles to capitalism and as the last phase of the transition from feudalism to capitalism. The Civil War in England is conceded to have been an aristocratic revolution, but the culture is still regarded as moving in a bourgeois direction. Political conditions were secured, it is argued, that allowed capitalism to operate through inflection of older forms and allowed the bourgeoisie to emerge within the nation. The feudal-aristocratic character of absolute monarchy has been much debated among marxists. France presents a particularly difficult problem because feudalism was not officially abolished until the Revolution and because capitalism can only triumph after the bourgeoisie have carried out their political revolution.

CULTURE AND MENTALITIES

To most theorists, capitalism is more than just an economic and social mechanism; it is an ideology whose ideals can motivate individuals to act. Capitalism can be defined as an imposed culture with prescribed patterns of behavior; the mode of production becomes a pluralistic lifestyle that commodifies all things. Some historians have argued that a national capitalist culture was created in England by the secularization of religion and the fragmentation of the customary moral economy. Capitalism has also been identified with psychological drives, with a unique attitude of mind, and with specific ends. Schumpeter thought that capitalism created a mentality compatible with itself.

George Simmel argued that in a capitalist society money is more than a medium of exchange and a repository of purchasing power; it is the measure of all things and the only measure of worth. Individuals have complete freedom, but all relationships and qualities are expressed in the common denominator of money, in quantitative and not qualitative terms, since only the measurable is regarded as real. Value is objictified by exchange that converts substantive values into divisible money values.

Marx and the critical theorists argued more broadly that capitalism made a fetish of money and goods and regarded the production of goods not as a means, but as an end in itself. Man is alienated from his essence and the relationship between humans and their labor is treated as a material relationship between things. Capital itself is alienated labor, objectified and reified as an external force. Value becomes intrinsic to every commodity without regard for the labor content in its production. Goods can be possessed at a distance and have more value as symbols than in use. Later versions of this theory identify capitalism with commercialized mass culture, with a world dominated by commodities and bereft of personal or public meaning.

The transition from feudalism to capitalism has been detected in every facet of culture. Capitalism is alleged to have generated the mental attitude of modern science and medicine. Literature, it has been argued, was dominated by awareness of the capitalist experience. Book production in England is alleged to have passed from an archaic economy of gift exchange and aristocratic patronage to a bourgeois culture of print in a self-regulating literary marketplace. The content and themes of drama are interpreted as allegories of the market; the theater replays the struggle between a customary and a capitalist culture. Literary theorists discuss the "poetics of nascent capitalism" and interpret the lists of traded commodities in the commercial manuals as icons bearing a subliminal message that they be acquired. The rise of the novel is directly attributed to economic individualism. Capitalism is alleged to have commodified both time and space; the universe became mechanical instead of organic, and the uncertainty of linear evolution replaced the security of cyclical development.

The most famous idealist theory of capitalism is Weber's Protestant Ethic. Weber believed that events could have intellectual causes, that a set of beliefs could determine both the outlook and the conduct of a society. Capitalism could only emerge after the idea had been invented. Weber's spirit of capitalism had initially been formulated by Sombart, who equated capitalism with both rational profit-maximizing and a system of production that revolutionized the work patterns of traditional society. Sombart also regarded the end of capitalism as noneconomic; however rational the means, the objective was not the utilitarian satisfaction of economic wants but the irrational pursuit of power and moral status. Weber and Sombart both equated capitalism with two, not altogether compatible, attitudes—rationality and asceticism.

Where Weber differed from Sombart was in his emphasis on religion, that the spirit of capitalism was a secularized by-product of Calvinist teaching on predestination and the calling. He freely admitted that acquisitiveness was an ancient human trait, but he argued that endless accumulation acquired a new and more effective motor in the early modern period, that it became a duty, an end in itself. Profit was maximized through rational calculation, not through speculation, entrepreneurial adventurism, privileges, or monopoly. Free labor was organized rationally for the irrational end of acquisition. Worldly asceticism—that is, thrift, self-denial, and awareness of time—benefited both production and accumulation.

The most important change in mentality, in Weber's view, was the introduction of the work ethic, which countered the elasticity of effort and preference for leisure that in the past had reduced output at the margin. Weber conceded that precapitalist societies had accounting methods, rationality, and acquisitive entrepreneurs; what they lacked, he argued, until after the Protestant Reformation was the notion of work as a vocation or duty.

In later life in his *General Economic History*, Weber played down the role of ideas in permitting and encouraging capitalism and recognized the importance of many other factors, including the growth of demand for goods. To modern theorists, more concerned with demand than with supply, the essence of capitalism is not frugal asceticism, but hedonistic consumerism, driven by fashion rather than necessity. It has been argued that in the eighteenth century Weberian deferred gratification collapsed into spending, into an insatiable, single-minded, irrational desire for goods. The consumption that was intrinsic to capitalism was based not on social utility but on individual sentiments, dreams, and delusions. In this theory, capitalism created a consuming public composed of isolated individuals who wished to display purchasing power, acquire personal meaning and social identity, and win the approbation of third parties.

Weber also recognized in his later work that capitalism was a historical continuum, that the market was created over time by profit-seeking entrepreneurs, not by ascetic bureaucrats. All theories of capitalism emphasize the importance of individualism—individual rights, the idea of self, the pursuit of self-interest. In an enterprise culture, Weberian rationality has to be combined with boldness and imagination. Some theorists have therefore emphasized the willingness to take risks; others have regarded profit not as expropriation of surplus labor but as a premium for innovation earned by those willing to write off old fixed assets. Schumpeter combined Austrian marginal utility theory with the traditions of the German Historical School to produce a dynamic theory of capitalism. He deplored the separation of economics and sociology and applauded Weber's efforts to combine the two subjects as *sozialökonomik*; the individual, he stressed, decides when and where to invest even though society produces the surplus. Clusters of entrepreneurs in bursts of innovation create new production functions by destroying old routines. To later theorists of entrepreneurship, only the free capitalist market can provide an opportunity for discovery.

CAPITALISM AS PROCESS

The core element of most theories of capitalism is economic change. When historians and sociologists talk about the rise of capitalism, they usually have in mind the economic development of the West. The idea that economic growth occurred in progressive evolutionary stages dates back to the Enlightenment. The first chronicler of the transition from primitive, self-sufficient feudalism to mercantile capitalism was, in fact, Adam Smith, who, of course, wrote before the Industrial Revolution. Marx retained Smith's growth model virtually intact, though he identified each stage with a change in the mode of production and in the relationship between capital and labor. Because he wished to highlight the role of capital and downplay the role of technology, Marx regarded industrialization as the final stage of capitalism.

The theory of evolution through stages was adopted by the German Historical School in preference to the ahistorical abstractions of Classical Economics; specific epochs were identified with a total economic system, each based on a distinctive institution. Sombart, for example, distinguished chronologically between early, high, and late capitalism, allocating to each stage its own value system, worldview, organization, and productive process.

Henri Pirenne believed that national economies grew out of urban economies, but his stages of growth were equated not with economic systems, but with individual capitalists, by which he meant rootless, calculating, speculative entrepreneurs. Pirenne thought that each stage of historical development had its own group of entrepreneurs, because the successful always abandoned business for rentiership, and because societies oscillated continuously between phases of economic freedom and interventionism. Pirenne's thesis of entrepreneurial discontinuity can be applied to the economic leadership of nations whose rise and decline relative to each other has a distinctive curve. According to Cardwell's law of interrupted progress, no society can sustain its technological or economic leadership forever. N. S. B. Gras, who identified capitalism with businessmen employing capital productively, also envisaged a progressive increase in the scale and sophistication of business organization from petty trade to commerce, industry, and finance.

Although stage theories are linear, they are not necessarily continuous or progressive. Marx prophesied that capitalism would eventually succumb to its own internal contradictions, to a falling rate of profit, to over-production and under-consumption. Ricardo's law of diminishing returns metamorphosed into the law of diminishing marginal utility. Schumpeter considered that stationary capitalism was impossible, that capitalism was inherently unstable and cyclical while able to absorb shocks and transform itself. His theory of entrepreneurship was in essence a theory of punctuated equilibrium with short bursts of rapid change rather than incremental growth. Conflict theory envisions a continuous struggle to preserve equilibrium in a capitalist economy.

The question of when, where, and how capitalism emerged has primarily been a concern for marxist theorists, among whom it has provoked a long debate. It is generally agreed that England became the first capitalist society in the seventeenth century, even though London was not the quintessential bourgeois city. The United Provinces, on the other hand, are classified by Eric Hobsbawm as an economy of feudal business, even though they dominated the world economy. Some marxists have conceded that capitalism was not a historical imperative and that the transition to capitalism may only have occurred in England. As a small concession to the undeniable growth of agricultural production and the long-lived supremacy of the landed class, some contemporary marxists have embraced the concept of "agrarian capitalism." Others, following Hilferding, have advanced theories of finance or state monopoly capitalism.

A more important issue is the relationship not between feudalism and capitalism but between capitalism and that other great discontinuity in orthodox histories of the Western world—the Industrial Revolution. This transition has attracted less debate and many have chosen to blur the distinction between capitalism and industrialization. Ernest Gellner, for example, has envisaged a leap directly from an agrarian to an industrial society. The United States, it has been alleged, moved from barbarism to decadence without becoming a civilization. To Pirenne, the Industrial Revolution was just a more intense form of earlier commercial development. One school of economic historians has replaced the old model of rapid industrialization driven by technological innovation with a model of gradual reduction over time in the proportion of the population engaged in agriculture. Others have discovered several Industrial Revolutions and postmodernists employ the term *postindustrial capitalism.*

In short, many concepts of capitalism have emerged with both real and symbolic attributes, each based on different formulas and many of them deliberately vague and ambiguous. Whether defined as an economic system, a social structure, or a set of attitudes, capitalism is a process rather than an event, defined in terms of function and values rather than in quantitative terms. It constitutes both a pattern of economic behavior and a set of ideas governing that behavior.

Does the idea of capitalism in any of its overlapping forms serve as a useful tool for comprehending the transition to modernity? Do any of the variant theories, when tested against empirical evidence, describe historical reality or explain the comparative development of the world? If not, then why has the idea survived so long and been so widely employed?

2

PRODUCTION
AND EXCHANGE

The main problem with the idea that capitalism emerged at a particular historical moment is that it is hard to find a precapitalist
economy. All human societies exchange surplus commodities, invest
capital, and maximize returns in terms of their specific cultural values.
Land, tools, and knowledge—all essential elements of the economic
infrastructure—can be regarded as capital assets. Although the influence of the market can be restrained by geographical isolation, political interference, or cultural inhibition, it has rarely been totally suppressed or ignored. Market capitalism appears as old as civilization
and is recognizable even in primitive societies.

Nor do economies fit into easily defined historical stages of
development such as agricultural, commercial, industrial, and financial capitalism. To Marx, the feudal economy was distinguished from
a capitalist economy by self-sufficiency and by production for the
household, not the market. Peasants held their land by service, not for
a money rent. In fact, most features of preindustrial capitalism can be
found in the medieval economy and many at a much earlier date. Nor

did one type of capitalism supersede another as a dominant form; they all coexisted, overlapped, and were interdependent.

Capitalist institutions were not, however, equally important in all periods and cultures. Both quantitative and qualitative changes in economic organization occurred over time. The market might be ubiquitous, but its degree of integration and dominance has varied. Some financial practices and methods of production date only from the modern era. Capitalism may be an abstract economic construct, but if it is manifested in history, it can be measured and empirically tested.

MARKET EXCHANGE

A central theme throughout human history is the continuous extension of the division of labor and the widening, deepening, and sectoral integration of the market. The exchange system is not rigid or monolithic in structure. Markets can function by barter without a bullion-based currency and without the value of goods being expressed in self-regulating prices; in their search for equilibrium, markets are inherently unstable, oscillating between glut and scarcity and subject to short- and long-term cyclical fluctuations.

Yet the general principles of the market are timeless. Specialization by function allows producers to increase output at lower cost and to achieve economies of scale. Market centralization improves communications between buyers and sellers and thereby reduces transaction costs. Competition matches supply to demand and equalizes prices. Uncertainty creates opportunity for profit. Trade permits the substitution of resources.

One school has argued that the market did not dominate preindustrial societies. To Karl Polanyi, markets were peripheral in early economies that exchanged goods through symmetrical reciprocity, not through centralized redistribution. Resources were allocated by social and political institutions; householders produced for their own use without reference to market price.

Other scholars have, however, demonstrated that primitive societies were familiar with the concept of exchange value. Market exchange has been discovered in all the ancient civilizations, from Mesopotamia onward. It has been shown that prices were not always fixed by the polity, that private capital did exist alongside public assets. Ancient Athens and Rome had a full-fledged market economy with durable economic institutions. The markets created by Islam and the medieval Italian and German cities embraced the whole known world and exchanged cheap, bulky commodities such as timber, salt, grain, wine, and minerals as well as luxury silks and spices.

Nonetheless, the development of the market in stages over time was uneven, erratic, and incomplete. A hierarchy of different markets existed—regional, national, and international. Early societies, like medieval England, could have active commodity markets but weaker factor markets allocating land or labor. Preindustrial economies did not really have autonomous markets. Monopolistic institutions weakened or eliminated competition. Markets were too separated by distance and time to provide adequate information to participants. Labor costs were high, diffused, and inelastic. Before the Industrial Revolution, markets could not operate in the classical sense; the premodern world was less rational and optimistic. Medieval landed estates were commercialized, but they were managed as political and social entities, not as businesses. In preindustrial societies, the market economy coexisted with payments in kind, self-sufficiency, and forced allocation of resources; they were dual economies that were not fully integrated.

The structure of international trade was changed by massive European colonization of the world from the sixteenth century onward and by the geographical transfer of commodities and centers of production. Capitalism's center of gravity shifted from the Mediterranean to the Atlantic. Regional and national economies were tied to distant markets by complex multilateral trading patterns. The volume of international transactions increased and the price to consumers of several staples fell. In England, the gains from trade at the margin were substantial: by 1700, exports represented 8 to 9 percent of the National Income and supported 20 percent of the population. But there was no world economy until the twentieth century. So long as transport costs remained high, goods produced locally (even imitations) always had a price advantage. Regular needs could only be satisfied regionally by rural industry.

The most important market was in fact the domestic market. In England the towns became large-scale distribution centers for food, fuel, raw materials, and discretionary consumer goods and had sophisticated housing markets. The metropolitan market was a national market. The main difference between the medieval and the modern economy was not employment of capital but a more focused and less intermittent demand. The slow growth of aggregate income always limited the level and rate of growth of demand. In a labor-intensive economy, real wages could not simultaneously be low enough to keep the production cost of goods competitive and high enough to stimulate demand. In England, the domestic market was sufficiently unified and large by the eighteenth century to justify specialization of production and distribution. But it was the social and economic structure that determined income distribution, which in turn determined purchasing power and consumption—not the market.

FINANCE

A capitalist economy presupposes both that sufficient capital has been accumulated to meet needs and that financial institutions have the capacity to transfer that capital to entrepreneurs to float new businesses. Without capital markets to manage capital flows and hire and sell productive assets, savings cannot be converted into investment capital and there can be no rentier capitalists. The essence of finance capitalism is the creation of fictitious money through the advance of credit.

Capital formation has been continuous throughout history, and there has always been a capitalist class in the sense that a tiny minority of any population owned or controlled the majority of capital assets. A low level of profits and savings and a low net reproducible capital-output ratio combined with a high cost of maintaining fixed assets to slow the rate of net capital formation before the Industrial Revolution. The view of the price historian Earl J. Hamilton, that the monetary inflation of the sixteenth century generated high profits as wages lagged behind prices, is no longer tenable. But a steady decline in the level of interest rates in early modern England and France suggests both a reduction in risk and growth in the capital supply. In the Netherlands, the capital stock increased by a factor of fifty between 1500 and 1650 and the rate of interest fell from 10 percent to under 4 percent. The growth of capitalism was delayed less by shortages of capital than by limited opportunities for profitable investment.

The credit system, including the use of financial instruments like the bill of exchange (which transferred funds through third parties), was of great antiquity. The trading systems of the Islamic and medieval world had a highly sophisticated remittance system. By the sixteenth century, the provision of credit was a dominant feature of most transactions. What changed in the seventeenth century was the efficiency and scope of the mechanism by which resources were borrowed or anticipated. The introduction of stock markets during the seventeenth century, with assignable shares and specialized brokerage services, improved the liquidity and mobility of capital and created the possibility of permanent funded public debts and of arbitrage between prices in different markets. As transactions became more secure and the level of confidence rose, capital assets were represented by paper instruments rather than by commodities. Now, subject to speculative crises such as the South Sea Bubble and Law's Scheme, it was possible to create credit on the basis of expectations.

The most visible instrument of financial capitalism was the bank. Banking functions can be identified in early societies, and medieval Italian financiers invented and refined many of the core features of modern banks. Most early deposit banks in Europe were, however, exchange institutions with an urban and not a national base. The Wisselbank of Amsterdam did not issue notes and was conservative in its expansion of credit. Although anticipated in various ways, the foundation of the Bank of England in 1694 after the establishment of Parliamentary sovereignty in 1688 created a different financial institution that was tied to the fiscal needs and the taxing power of the state. In preindustrial economies, however, bankers were neither promotional nor speculative capitalists. They were more active in collectively underwriting public loans than in providing unsecured advances to industry for fixed and working capital.

Joint investment with active or sleeping (simple investors) partners is also a practice of great antiquity. Complex companies of shareholders with huge capital assets and multifarious business interests date from the thirteenth century in medieval Italy. The legal fiction of the corporation gave companies institutional, if not economic, permanence. Individuals could buy, sell, and transfer shares without dissolving the business entity. The scale of enterprise increased continuously; the leading international company of each era was larger than its predecessor. During the seventeenth century, water companies, public banks, and giant trading corporations, like the English and Dutch East India Companies, emerged with permanent joint stocks and an ever-changing body of shareholders drawn from the general population. Public insurance corporations date from the eighteenth century. Ultimately, the economy would be dominated by giant firms run neither by capitalists nor by the market but by bureaucracies of specialized executives.

Such institutions, which divorced ownership from management, were, however, the exception even in the early decades of industrialization. Even highly capitalized industries, like coal mining, functioned without public stockholders. The majority of joint-stock companies that were floated (often fraudulently) by promoters failed. It was not until the Railway Age that shares became a form of property in their own right and that the corporation acquired a life of its own. Only slowly did control of the means of production pass from individual capitalist owners to technocrats and professional managers. A corporate culture based on institutional loyalty and internal discipline emerged late as a long-term consequence of industrialization.

Early historians of capitalism, like Sombart, placed great emphasis on the adoption of double-entry accounting as an instrument of rational profit maximization. Weber identified capitalism with rational, permanent enterprises governed by methodical routines. Without question, most accounting methods and numerous other business techniques were invented in medieval Italy with some borrowings from Islam. Tuscan accounting by the fourteenth century was able to distinguish the capital of a partnership or firm from the wealth of the partners. These facts are hard to reconcile with the view that capitalism developed in the sixteenth century. Sombart, who was aware of Italian precocity in this respect, had to argue rather disingenuously that the Italians did not seek to maximize their profits.

In fact, there is no obvious connection between double-entry accounting and capitalism, which owed much more to developments in public finance. Few businessmen employed the technique or knew how to define real cost or verify the current value of their resources or project future cash flow. Preindustrial firms did not employ budgeting, forecasting, market research, or inventory control as management tools. The accounts of the joint stock companies reveal little understanding of the term *capital*. Early accountancy was not really mathematical and it played a passive and symbolic role in business. Information was gathered and displayed for ritual assurance, to create myths, and to bolster decisions that had already been made on inadequate knowledge.

PRODUCTION

Although economic growth is usually identified with industrial production, no economy can expand without an efficient agricultural sector. Even a heavily urbanized economy like that of the Netherlands had a capital-intensive agriculture. In sixteenth-century England, land appreciated in value as the population increased and common fields were enclosed. From the seventeenth century onward, helped by greater investment, the productivity of English agriculture improved continuously. As early as 1700, England had no peasants and only half the workforce was employed in agriculture; despite some pockets of subsistence agriculture, farmers produced for the market, land was treated as a commodity, and there was an integrated rural market. These changes have been categorized as agrarian capitalism.

Neomarxists have come to accept the idea that agriculture can be capitalist and produce a bourgeoisie. It has been applied both to England and to the English colonies in America, which, to some historians, never passed through a precapitalist stage. But the notion of agrarian capitalism is not easy to reconcile with traditional marxist teaching on the relations of production and the formation and conflict of classes. English agriculture was in fact transformed by demographic pressure and by the market with some government support rather than by any basic change in the mode of production. Many landowners were neither feudal lords nor active capitalists, but rentiers who did not control agricultural production.

Although some towns had a parasitic role as centers of administration and leisure, others retained their importance as centers of manufacture and of consumption. Demand was projected outward from the resident population; export industries could be founded initially on the consumption of luxury goods by urban elites. But town and country developed in unison; the desire of farmers for goods supplied by the towns acted as an incentive to improve their income from agriculture.

Before the Industrial Revolution, commerce served as the catalyst for economic change. Production was controlled by merchants, not by industrialists. The capitalist acted as a middleman between producer and consumer, supplying raw materials to artisans both in the towns and in the countryside. The rural workforce, particularly in pastoral regions, combined industrial with agricultural occupations. In preindustrial England, with its limited technology and small-scale production, agriculture and industry were linked through the domestic system. In all but a few specialized trades, the merchant capitalist undermined the self-sufficiency of the artisan and the guild structure of manufacture. The principal concern was efficiency of organization, not growth of output.

Most commodities, including capital goods like housing, were produced on a small scale by small units. By the end of the seventeenth century smelting, dyeing, brewing, and alum and salt manufacture were fueled by coal; the blast furnace and the slitting mill had transformed the iron industry. Piecemeal technological innovation, often by immigrants, had improved the manufacture and processing of textiles, sugar, and paper. But most industries were organically based, dependent on water power and vegetable products. Although the location of raw materials and channels of communication encouraged some regional specialization, production was concentrated in fixed plants only in a handful of industries, such as naval shipbuilding, smelting, and alum manufacture.

Whereas agriculture was limited by supply, industry was limited by demand. Without mass consumption, only the state could provide a consistent, large-scale market for a particular commodity, whether guns or butter. Nor was the technology yet available to systematically mechanize production or increase output per capita. Costs were not reduced through innovation nor was productivity increased by substituting capital for labor.

A distinction can be drawn between commercial and industrial capitalism. Land constituted the main long-term capital asset before the Industrial Revolution. Fixed capital was relatively unimportant except in land reclamation and drainage, shipbuilding, mining, and heavy industry. Working capital usually circulated in stocks of raw materials, unfinished goods, inventory, and credit. Merchant capitalists were prepared to take risks and they acknowledged the importance of putting money to work. But success was unpredictable and so they often chose to hedge their bets rather than maximize their returns. The primary purpose of business organization was to pool and limit risk. Investors preferred short-term and liquid investments; inertia slowed their response to investment opportunities and they were reluctant to shorten the life of fixed assets by innovation.

Through misallocation and underutilization of resources, capitalists deviated from the optimum path of development. The struggle for markets meant that capital flowed where it could make the best marginal return, not necessarily where it was most productive. Often it was employed in usury, purchase of office, or lending to governments rather than in trade or industry. Profit levels, adjusted for risk, were often no higher than the prevailing rate of interest, and social overhead investment did not yield an immediate return on investment. The growth of capitalism might depend on a rise in net investment and on reinvestment in productive facilities, but investment opportunities were limited and the costs often exceeded the benefits.

RELATIVE CHANGE

The idea that capitalism emerged only in early modern Europe does not square with the historical facts. If it is equated with a functioning market for goods or credit, it is visible at an early date in practically all cultures. Even isolationist societies, like Tokugawa Japan and Ming China, had cities, mines, specialized markets, paper money, a credit system, and bills of exchange. Mughal India had huge foreign and internal markets, double-entry bookkeeping, financial instruments, and large-scale manufacturing.

The long-term trend was certainly away from simple self-sufficiency and communal distribution toward a sophisticated market economy. This was an unavoidable consequence of the search for greater efficiency, for a higher ratio of output to input of energy. But different economies evolved at different rates of speed and without sudden or permanent discontinuities. The extension of the market, the division of labor, and the creation of a credit system were all products of a continuous and incremental process of evolution. Over the centuries, the scale and structure of economic activity was transformed more than once with a consequential increase in levels of wealth.

Before the Industrial Revolution, however, this represented more of the same—larger companies, wider markets, a more complex payments mechanism, greater concentrations of capital, and the faster circulation of goods. Unlike industrialization, which can be defined and periodized in terms of output and productivity, capitalism is difficult to standardize and quantify. Nor is it always clear when quantitative change should be regarded as qualitative, since only the former can be measured objectively. Capital was, moreover, only one of many factors in economic development, some of which, such as population and technology, were exogenous to the economy. The scale of economic activity certainly increased over time, but the changes were relative rather than absolute, changes of degree, not of kind. The fundamental character and direction of capitalism remained the same, even though it grew stronger and developed at a faster pace.

The economic growth of nations has not been linear, regular, uniform, or balanced. Some early capitalist economies failed to industrialize and others deindustrialized or decentralized in response to competition and market risk. In the seventeenth century, Italy gave up banking and the manufacture of textiles for export and became an agricultural economy, because it lacked the capacity to compete with the Atlantic powers; the Dutch followed a similar path in the eighteenth century. Others diverged from the norm: England and Holland were little affected by the demographic and economic crisis that hit much of Western Europe in the seventeenth century. Some societies experienced a retrogressive cycle of development. In Eastern Europe, which had a different land/labor ratio from its Western counterpart, feudal services were reimposed in the early modern period; the Junkers became agrarian capitalists with serf labor.

It is not unreasonable to associate the rise of capitalism with the preindustrial European economy. The world economy was, for example, created by European exploration and colonization, which sharply differentiated the economic development of the West from that of Islam and China. The Great Discoveries reduced the man-land ratio in Europe and indirectly monetized the fiscal and international trading system with American bullion. But preindustrial economies had few defenses against the Malthusian specter of population exceeding resources, and they were labor-intensive and poor. Their commodity and financial markets might be capitalist, but with limited sources of energy, low productivity, and a predominately agricultural workforce, they could not achieve mass production and consumption.

Full-fledged capitalism had to be based on an increase in demand as well as supply; on a larger volume of continuous, standardized production; on higher real incomes; and on discretionary purchasing power, economies of scale, lower unit costs, and the separation of retail distribution from production. Mass markets, rapid technological change, and the divorce of ownership from management are all modern developments. If a capitalist economy is defined as one in which total economic output is produced by capitalist methods, then capitalism must be identified with the Industrial Revolution.

3

FROM STATUS TO CONTRACT

The earliest societies with their limited resources had to restrain individual desires; they could only survive through cohesive action and
mutual aid. It was taken for granted that society was an indivisible and
organic whole; land and labor were allocated by kinship and by political obligation, not by the market. In stages, however, over a long period
of time, the economy was separated from society; social and political
institutions were more subjected to market forces. New social groups
emerged wherever and whenever trade, urbanization, government
favor, or war created new wealth. Those societies that embraced capitalism became more mobile; their members were differentiated by merit
and performance as well as by birth because the market recognizes no
distinction of persons. In the West, the conjugal, nuclear family became
more private and domesticated while group-based kinship and communal obligations declined in importance; individuals eventually acquired
the right to choose freely whom they married.

The community increasingly took second place to a new conceptual entity—the nation-state—which was governed by a centralized
bureaucracy drawing on the resources of an integrated fiscal system. If

the early modern period witnessed the birth of capitalism, it also witnessed the universal growth of bureaucracy, the military revolution, and in some states a financial revolution, which enabled governments to anticipate revenue on a massive scale. Both in theory and in legal practice, individual rights acquired greater recognition and force; in England, the concept of private property was clarified while government interference to protect the moral economy became less common.

The transition to a capitalist society was not, however, completed smoothly. The new society was still legitimated by old values and the patriarchal system survived the triumph of contract. Kinship connections retained their importance, and national interests did not supersede those of community and region. The claims of merit still had to compete with inherited status and privilege. The role of capitalism in state formation was also equivocal. It is difficult to determine whether the state created the market or the market created the state; whether stability was created by government or vice versa. Bureaucracy was to prove stronger than individualism; property rights were far from absolute.

SOCIAL DIFFERENTIATION

Undoubtedly, higher levels of capitalization did reduce the number of self-employed craftsmen who merely owned their tools and a shop and did increase the number of wage earners. Entrepreneurial middlemen divided production from distribution and undermined the cooperative guild system, with its monopolistic tendencies and restrictive practices. The expansion of the market created an international division of labor; new technologies made old skills redundant. The capitalist was sometimes a financier without roots operating in a disembodied market.

Yet it was not so much intensified capitalization of the economy as the division of labor that, by promoting functional specialization and diversification, destroyed the organic society and the integrated community. Industrialization, rather than urbanization, created anomie, fragmentation, the loss of occupational status, and a proletariat. Towns, it is true, had greater occupational mobility and frequency of contact with outsiders than tightly knit, homogeneous, rural communities. But the stability and cohesion of agrarian society was also undermined by demographic change and migration.

All societies differentiate their members and allocate them both specific and discretionary roles; social and economic inequality is well nigh universal. Economic growth and greater prosperity can reduce the unequal distribution of resources. But ruling elites usually strive to maintain the old distribution of income between groups, even when real income increases. Simon Kuznets has argued that economic growth increases inequality of incomes because the rewards of improved productivity are unevenly distributed to those whose particular skills match demand. Conflict over the allocation of benefits occurred in all societies, but it was accentuated by the growth of capitalism, whose very success highlighted social divisions and economic differences and generated new wants and expectations. The doctrine of an overall harmony of interests lacked conviction when social groups were clearly polarized by earnings and economic function as well as by gender and age.

In preindustrial societies there was from an early date an independent middle group (of farmers as well as artisans) between the wealthy landed and business elites and the mass of families living at or just above subsistence level. The middle class, as has often been said, is always rising, at least in Western Europe. But the rate of social change accelerated in early modern Europe, parallel with the development of capitalism, and this created new tensions and new social identities. The history of the Netherlands demonstrates that a bourgeoisie could emerge and dominate a culture without an Industrial Revolution.

In England, the first industrial nation, it can be argued, however, that the industrial bourgeoisie never wrested political or social hegemony from the landed class. Class formation was never as simple as the marxist model would suggest. The infinite gradations of property ownership in a capitalist society blurred class distinctions. Wealth was rarely accepted as a self-justifying end, and it did not necessarily serve as the only or even the most important criteria for social differentiation. Capitalists sought prestige rather than profit and welcomed absorption through gentrification into the old order. Salaries, as distinct from profits, identified the service industries as well as the proletariat. The professions based their independent, self-governing status not on capital, but on intellect, training, and formal paper qualifications that were impartially assessed, universally recognized, and ubiquitously enforced.

The relationship between capitalism and the basic unit of society, the family, is equally uncertain. The nuclear family has a long history in Western Europe and Alan MacFarlane has associated it with the early growth of individualism and capitalism in England. It is true that the nuclear family encouraged delayed gratification and capital accumulation, that both the separation of the household from work and the retreat from community into the domestic family promoted business enterprise. Loyalty to the family was less obstructive to economic individualism than loyalty to a fraternity, a craft, or kin, any of whom might be competitors. Individual members were mobile and could articulate and negotiate their interests rationally and efficiently without community interference. The decline in arranged marriages and the greater role played by affection in choosing a spouse did coincide with the successful assertion of individual property rights. Market forces and social mobility destroyed ties of lineage even in sheltered societies, like Japan.

On the other hand, bourgeois families tended to practice partible inheritance and disperse their communal assets, whereas landed families accumulated and transferred their estates from generation to generation. The greater the prospects for individual mobility and advancement with security, the weaker the family. The nuclear family always coexisted with kinship; kin networks were not eliminated by either individualism or by the growth of industrial cities. The extended family was not only compatible with, but helped to create, the market economy. Increased mobility enhanced the value of kin, as individuals migrated toward economic opportunities and away from their families of birth.

Usually, the common interests of the preindustrial family took precedence over the interests of individuals; most decisions were group decisions. But the marxist notion that love could only occur in bourgeois social relations is easily refuted. The idea of romantic love predates and does not require a capitalist economy. Nor did the development of capitalism fundamentally alter the theoretical structure of the family. The doctrine of male dominance and female submission was frequently challenged and often ignored in particular marriages; the duties of parenthood were shared between husband and wife while widows exercised considerable power. But European societies remained patriarchal in principle, if not in practice, even after industrialization. In the long run, the role and functions of the family were transformed less by capitalism than by the growth of the state, which gradually usurped many of the family's traditional functions—from education to welfare.

PUBLIC POLICY

It is important to remember that economics was originally termed *political economy*. The state has been as much a benefactor as a beneficiary of capitalism; politicians propose and markets dispose. Only an organized polity can unify and centralize the economy; guarantee order, security of communications, and property; and maintain the infrastructure, the currency, and the credit system. Governments formulate and codify laws, reduce interpersonal and intergroup conflict, bridge internal divisions, and reconcile differences.

Although they have on occasion acted like capitalists seeking maximum returns, governments have usually defined their objectives and responsibilities more widely. Until the eighteenth century the English state was paternalistic, upholding the family values of the household and the corporate values of the guilds. Because its very survival was threatened by disorder, the monarchy protected its subjects from starvation and unemployment, regulated the prices and quality of goods, allocated labor, prohibited or regulated usury, and discouraged disruptive actions by entrepreneurs. In sixteenth-century England, for example, Sir Thomas Smith recognized the role of self-interest, that the economy was driven by private vices, but he did not regard the economy as self-regulating and argued that the Crown must act as arbiter. This remained the dominant view until Adam Smith launched his attack on what he termed the *mercantile system*. Few economic historians now subscribe, however, to the view, initially propagated by the German Historical School, that mercantilism constituted a coherent ideology or system. Government intervention in the economy usually had little impact. Paternalistic policies were jettisoned in England once food supplies became more secure and once faith in the market increased at the end of the seventeenth century. Government regulation of the economy continued, but it was now intended to help, not to resist capitalism.

Capitalism is traditionally associated with representative government and with decentralized, maritime nation states, rather than with autocracy or with landlocked, pluralistic, territorial empires. The earliest centers of capitalism were the politically independent city-states that were controlled by businessmen and not subject to an external, regulatory bureaucracy. In Europe, the modern state is usually identified with the bourgeoisie, with liberty and property, natural rights, and equitable taxation; political and constitutional reform is postulated as a precondition of capitalism.

Before the Revolution of 1688 in England, the threat of arbitrary action raised the level of risk; kings could repudiate government debts and debase the currency. Once Parliament achieved political and financial supremacy, a national economy was able to emerge, governed by contract. In absolutist France, on the other hand, a full-fledged market economy was obstructed by regionalism and aristocratic opposition, though Charles Tilly has also argued that heavy taxation of the peasantry forced them into the market and that state fiscalism created a bourgeois officer class.

Political stability was certainly essential for economic development; government by consensus was more efficient than populist or confrontational politics. But capitalism could flourish without either laissez-faire attitudes or participatory democracy. Only those countries with an entrepôt trade, like the Dutch, or with a clear lead over all their competitors, like the English, were likely to favor free trade. All the free cities and urban republics were eventually absorbed by nation-states and territorial empires. The dominant form of the fiscal state in ancien regime Europe was absolute monarchy.

Even England benefited from having strong, centralized government. Although the East India Company was virtually an independent power in India, with its own military muscle, the company had to share its profits with the political elite in England. The bourgeois state of marxist theory is little in evidence before the Industrial Revolution. The agents of political change were the landed and professional elite rather than the urban or industrial bourgeoisie. Meiji Japan built a capitalist economy on nationalism without a competitive market and without changing fundamental traditions.

No capitalist society could have emerged without political help. Only the state could safeguard private property, provide tariff protection, and finance the infrastructure of the economy through taxation. Governments created monopolies to avoid excess capacity and losses and to sustain the rate of return on invested capital. When the fixed costs of business were high, the state attempted to control markets by regulating the supply of raw materials as well as labor. It ventured where individual investors feared to tread and was expected to resolve the conflicts and mitigate the effects of structural economic change. In order to finance expensive global wars, governments had to anticipate and raise revenue through direct taxes on land and indirect taxes on consumption. This certainly enriched financiers and tax farmers, but it also circulated capital and redistributed wealth through transfer payments to receivers of interest. In England, businessmen had always been heavily involved in the collection and anticipation of public revenue. But it was the Financial Revolution of the 1690s, by creating a durable and open-ended system of public credit, that can be said to have capitalized the patronage and party system.

Nonetheless, close regulation of the economy by the state, as in Prussia or Colbertian France, was often counterproductive. Closed markets and cartels fostered inefficiencies; group decisions and divided responsibility discouraged innovation and alternative ideas. The political system had an inherent bias toward economic and social stagnation, because too many stood to lose from change; each interest group fought to maintain the conditions that had originally created it. Most states were able to mobilize greater resources when they discouraged corporate monopolies and encouraged capitalists to compete freely in the economy.

Weber and Schumpeter expected that capitalism would ultimately be stifled by either corporate or state bureaucracies. Weber in his later works emphasized the importance of institutions rather than ideas; in particular, he believed that bureaucracy and capitalism were both rooted in the rationalization of action and that this process was irreversible. Weber credited full time administrators with effecting the transition from feudalism, freeing land and labor, eliminating internal barriers, standardizing the currency, raising armies, advancing literacy, and annexing the cities. But he also thought that bureaucracy would reintroduce patrimonialism and that control of the state by a military bureaucracy was incompatible with commercial capitalism, as was demonstrated by the history of Islam and China.

The impersonal, formal, and universal character of bureaucracy and the addiction of corporations to monopoly certainly conflict directly with individualism and the free play of the market. When elites are autonomous, creative individuals tend to join those specialized cadres where their talents are most in demand. Large-scale, centralized administrations, on the other hand, offer less scope for initiative and flexibility and favor the long-term security and prestige of a predictable corporate ideology. Administrative skills do not vary much over time and most impersonal institutions develop covert structures that preserve intimacy. But the bureaucratic compulsion to systematize creates a self-perpetuating order.

The aims and methods of bureaucracy are different from those of the capitalist or entrepreneur. The bureaucrat does not welcome competition or the market but tries to reach a consensus and a balance between interest groups. He prefers to determine priorities by regulation; to ration by need; to distribute rather than create; to foster loyalty to the institution rather than to the individual or family; to emphasize discipline, precision, and duty; and to maintain continuity rather than to effect change.

Political support was essential to compete in the world economy because markets had to be captured and defended. Through privateering as well as open warfare the English invaded the spheres of influence and seized the trade of Spain, Holland, and France. The great imperial powers, like Spain in the late sixteenth century, were also great economic powers. Geopolitical conditions continuously altered world markets, which were subject to control by state monopolies and governed by a global balance of power. Even nominally independent states could be effectively subordinated by the terms of trade.

All the colonizing powers—Portugal, Spain, Holland, England, and France—wielded a big stick in America and Asia and annexed territory as booty. The Netherlands might have a federal system of government, but strong, aggressive support at the center was necessary to create and sustain the Dutch commercial empire. The great trading companies raised and used their own military and naval forces for both attack and defense, but they fundamentally relied on state protection against their enemies. England was unusual in that it established both a commercial and a territorial empire and was prepared to make a huge, long-term investment in sea power with a network of bases.

Capitalism was not necessarily advanced by either the military revolution or by imperialism. The gradual establishment of large permanent, professional, and technologically advanced armies and navies increased the authority of state bureaucracies and cleared the way for European domination of the world, but war was still labor-intensive and a drain on resources. Although governments were sometimes prepared to adopt economic policies and new technologies in order to win wars, they were driven by a desire to maximize their power and prestige, not the profits of their economies. States annexed the lands discovered by explorers and transplanted their domestic social institutions and population. The old attachment to community metamorphosed into nationalism. Most wars were fought to extend or defend territorial frontiers, not to produce wealth. Although the overall benefits of empire are difficult to assess, their profitability was short-lived; eventually, the cost of maintenance exceeded the returns.

PROPERTY AND CONTRACT

All theories of capitalism posit private property rights, that individuals can exclude others and legally own, exploit, alienate, and transfer their assets without restriction. A capitalist society by definition is one in which a majority of resources are controlled by individual property owners, not by society or the state. States, whether ancient or modern, that own all the land and are run by an all-powerful bureaucracy do not qualify as capitalist, even when they have exchange markets. When property is insecure and contracts cannot be easily enforced, transaction costs become too high for the market to function.

Property rights as well as loans and contracts were recognized as far back as Mesopotamia. Alan MacFarlane has argued against heavy opposition that rights of ownership and alienation (and thereby individualism) were established very early in English rural society. In England, the Common Law preferred efficiency to equity and was hostile to monopolies; the development of contract law and better remedies for creditors allowed market forces to operate efficiently. The doctrine of caveat emptor served as an alternative to regulation and protection.

This created some problems for Weber, who believed that Roman law had systematized and created the concept of ownership and the rational legal state whereas the English legal system did not meet his standards of rationality. He was obliged to argue that the law was adapted by judicial reasoning to legitimate a pecuniary system controlled by capitalist functionaries. Even so, property was as much a political as an economic right; property rights were often defended more vehemently by the poor than by the rich. The assertion that individuals have exclusive rights to property and should be free from external interference is relatively modern. Only in the nineteenth century was the paternalism of judges replaced by a laissez-faire approach and contract based on free choice.

Political society was originally seen as a corporate entity, a commonwealth of individuals sharing a common end, not as an aggregate of individuals with rights. Indeed, rights of ownership generated a conflict of values between the claims of the individual and those of the group. If capitalism was to survive, the new social and political structure had to be legitimized by credible arguments. Intellectual defenses of individual entitlement to property, as distinct from possession at the discretion of the state, can be found as early as the ancient world, but the classic, hedonistic doctrine that property is natural, not because it fulfills a final purpose, but because it is driven by human needs and desires, really dates from the seventeenth century. A restricted technical term was transformed into an abstract right; the machinations of the legal conveyancers were elevated by theorists into a blueprint for society. The most celebrated defender of property, John Locke, was indeed opposed to endless accumulation. Only in the first age of the world, he argued, was property appropriated by labor on the basis of natural right and subordinated to the right to life; after money had been introduced, property was based on utility and had to be regulated and restricted. But the liberal political theorists in practice sought to justify the inequalities of market society; the cultural hegemony of landowners created a law of property that protected the group but whose benefits flowed to individual families.

In fact, private property rights were always hedged with restrictions. Capital assets were usually held by institutions or families, not by individuals; exclusive rights were granted to groups. In the Middle Ages, the holding of markets and the hunting of game were prerogatives of lordship; the freedom to trade or even to work were privileges that excluded others. In England, the Common Law made primogeniture the dominant mode of transfer of real property and landed testators tried to bind their descendants to maintain the integrity of the family estate.

But the law of inheritance limited freedom of devise; both customary and civil law recognized the concept of community property and distributed movables more equally. Partible inheritance was the norm in America and in urban society. A reverence for private property did validate market forces, but the claims of distributive justice were not dismissed but simply deferred.

It would be a mistake to equate capitalism with any single legal system. The English Common Law, for all its virtues, was slow to address crucial issues at the heart of capitalism such as rights of assignment and the liability of passive investors in stocks. The rigidities of the law with regard to debt obligations had to be remedied by the equity courts. Since the principal beneficiaries of individual rights and the sanctity of contract were men, women had to seek protection from Chancery. Japan managed to build a capitalist society by relying on personal and group obligations instead of on contract.

CHANGE AND CONTINUITY

Human history has been shaped by contradictory forces that simultaneously seek and destroy equilibrium. The "civil society" created by capitalism was riven by numerous internal conflicts—between domesticity and work, between privilege and merit, between power and plenty, between dispersal and concentration, between maintenance and growth, between the creation and the distribution of wealth. The private sphere was never completely separated from or reconciled with the public sphere. There was constant tension between freedom and regulation, between allowing private individuals to make choices and intervening in the economy to promote the public interest. One inevitable consequence of the accumulation of resources in private hands was increased pressure for social justice and public welfare.

Capitalist societies did not conform to a simple, consistent model; they were hybrids of variant forms whose relative importance fluctuated. There was no linear progression from the simple to the complex; despite the addition and adaptation of new norms and methods, one social system did not replace another. Several sets of attitudes and values were current at the same time. Old practices and procedures were continued, sometimes under new names, and survived so long as they remained functional and competitive with new alternatives. Contractual relationships, which appeared well before the early modern period, modified but did not supersede a system based on status, patriarchy, and kinship. Although land ceased to be the only form in which major assets could be held and although the concept of private property emerged more clearly, England remained a traditional society in which the family remained the basic unit.

The scale of social and political change did increase dramatically over time, parallel with the economy. The naval and demographic power needed to sustain an empire in the eighteenth-century Atlantic was much greater than in the fourteenth-century Adriatic. The inclusive and consensual city-state gave way to the confrontational nation-state. But the real transformation of society came with industrialization, not capitalism. The world was controlled by power networks, not by capital.

Structural change was built into the system. Nothing lasts in the market or in politics, because needs and opportunities change and destabilize the system. Communal societies could only survive under conditions of demographic, political, and technological stagnation. The life span of empires, as of dominant economies, is finite. Sooner or later, the cost of defense and administration cannot be financed by expropriating new territory or taxing the inhabitants; bureaucratic lethargy overwhelms imperial administration. Few societies, whether capitalist or not, voluntarily embrace change. Established elites are fundamentally conservative and wish to perpetuate the status quo. The effects of capitalism were delayed, concealed, and diluted because people acted as though nothing had changed. What made the emergence of a capitalist society acceptable was the passage of time. Eventually, a generation matured that had no personal experience of any other way of life.

4

THE SPIRIT OF CAPITALISM

Capitalism has been credited with its own ethos and mentality, with specific traits of personality, and with learned, socially sanctioned behavior. Adam Smith, like others writing before the Industrial Revolution, thought that civility had displaced gentility in England, that mercantile concepts of justice and trust had superseded the military values of honor, chivalry, and heroism characteristic of a feudal regime.

The famous or infamous "spirit of capitalism" propagated by Sombart and Weber is more complex. It really combines three different attributes: the bourgeois ethos of thrift, work, discipline, and respect for time; the rational calculus of economic individualism; and the entrepreneurial willingness to innovate and take risks. Later historians have introduced the notion of a culture of capitalism in which the motivation and social roles of individuals are determined by material self-interest. Henri Sée thought that capitalism created Renaissance individualism.

In any culture, it is the value system that sanctions behavior, defines expectations, and provides a rationale for life. The cumulative impact of culture is subtle and deceptive, because the unconscious

47

assumptions that operate only become the grounds for judgment when individuals have a choice between alternatives. But it is culture that gives meaning to the anonymous abstraction of money and that influences the rate of innovation and the disposal of income.

Nonetheless, it is extremely difficult to demonstrate the mechanism by which social values become individual aspirations, to link values to actual behavior either in time or place. Personality is harder to duplicate than a role; changes in sentiments over time cannot easily be identified and calibrated. Different cultures might express emotions in different ways and accord them different degrees of importance, but the elementary human passions and drives have not changed fundamentally over time. The concept of individual identity has been detected as early as the fourteenth century. All cultures borrow and incorporate many aspects of the systems that they absorb or replace. Value systems relate to whoever values, not to the subject; they usually establish and then replicate the interests and preoccupations of the elite.

Projections of ideal communities cannot be equated with actual, historical societies. Even when what individuals ought or have to perform is formally expressed and enjoined in written custom or laws, it cannot be assumed that these rules were either accepted or obeyed. Usually, what was normally expected has to be inferred from isolated practices and literary sources, which are both contradictory and anecdotal. The bane of marxists are those historical characters who think like feudal lords or peasants, but behave like capitalists.

ETHOS

The numerous bourgeois virtues did not all appear at the same time or with the same intensity. Honesty, diligence, frugality, and asceticism were moral imperatives in precapitalist societies; the Benedictine

Order promulgated these economic virtues in the ninth century. Preindustrial societies with their limited resources were concerned with maximizing output and minimizing consumption. Attitudes toward saving certainly differ between cultures, some of which adopt a short-term approach and do not emphasize postponement of desires and sacrifices for the future. But thrift and the accumulation of property are found in most cultures, even in matrilineal societies with communal ownership of land, such as the Tolai of Melanesia.

The work ethic and greater consciousness of the value of time are, however, more recent developments. In preindustrial societies, the seasons determined the rhythm of work, which was constantly interrupted by voluntary and involuntary idleness. Even when improvements in technology relaxed constraints on an economy, the gains could be taken in leisure rather than in goods. The ritual cycles of agrarian communities outlived the economic and social circumstances that had originally created them. The transition to capitalism involved some degree of secularization of the religious impulse; individuals now strove to perform good works in this world rather than content themselves with the expectation of reward in the next world.

Several difficulties arise, however, when Weber's moral asceticism is equated with the spirit of capitalism. First, the work ethic was quite different from the profit motive. Hinduism, for example, never regarded exchange or usury as intrinsically immoral, but it did not esteem labor. The work ethic was more relevant to the Industrial Revolution, which needed disciplined, continuous factory labor, than to mercantile capitalism.

Second, Weber in later life identified rational asceticism more with bureaucracy than with capitalism. His ideal type of capitalism has been equated with the personality structure of the Prussian bureaucrat. Capital accumulation (which itself is subject to depreciation and redundancy of assets) cannot be simultaneously a means and an end. Weber posed too many paradoxes: that change was automatic and induced, that a sense of helplessness fortified the will to strive, that spontaneous conviction was compatible with objective self-awareness.

Third, it is doubtful whether economic actions can be closely associated with any specific ethos or motives. Weber conceded that religion was only one factor in promoting capitalism and that the principal role of ideas was to remove cultural obstacles to change. In fact, insofar as Protestant theology did accommodate capitalism, it was responding to and not initiating change. The principal reason why aliens and religious dissenters were disproportionately important in business is simply that they were excluded from alternative professions and occupations.

Some features of a market-based morality emerged at an early date. Although the medieval Church espoused the celebrated doctrine of the just price and denounced usury, the Scholastics often equated the just price with the market price under conditions of free competition and usury was permitted for charitable uses and when the return on capital was not free of risk. A few secular writers in the sixteenth and seventeenth centuries began to justify economic conduct in terms of a utilitarian, commercial ethic.

In the eighteenth century, however, the culture of the market visibly moved away from virtue toward envy, competition, consumption, and self-regard. The Stoic and Christian ethics fell out of fashion, despite a continuing fear of private interests. Bernard Mandeville, in his *Fable of the Bees,* could equate commercial society with civility, happiness, and progress and proclaim the sovereignty of the private consumer and his wants. Adam Smith believed that moral sentiments constituted a precondition of exchange, which was not impersonal but predicated on social interaction and the natural gregariousness as well as the selfish passions of humans. Laymen now felt that their material interests as individuals provided a better guide to conduct than obedience to civil society. In the new capitalist society morality rested less on conviction or on a sense of social responsibility and more on the market, which attached cost to violations.

Nonetheless, few writers, not even political arithmeticians like Sir William Petty, were enthusiastic apologists for capitalism. It is difficult to accept Locke as even an agrarian capitalist; he advocated neither ceaseless accumulation, nor a labor theory of exchange, nor a free-market economy. The emergence of a monied interest in England did little to shake the predominance of agrarian, anticapitalist values. Few were prepared to accept the logic of capitalism that money was the common denominator and the only determinant of worth because that leveled social distinctions. Chivalric values survived among the European nobility until the killing fields of World War I. In fact, an independent code of ethics, such as fiduciary obligations to investors, was essential to regulate behavior and sustain the market, which could not be governed solely by the search for maximum efficiency.

The majority of societies are achievement-motivated even when roles are ascribed and the economy is not capitalist. Actions by individuals need goals, which have to be evaluated and chosen. Value systems may be contradictory, but the interplay between individuals and the prevailing culture has regularities that determine social roles. Individual autonomy can be reconciled with social conditioning by keeping the same goals but changing the means.

The anxiety that fosters self-denial and discipline can be generated by either guilt or shame. An extended system of loyalties and obligations, as in Japan, can produce the same effect as the desire for individual self-realization. Pride can have the same impact on motivation as acquisitiveness, though the desire to preserve order and dignity can nullify the healthy challenge of competition and lead to uncritical, complacent consensus.

ECONOMIC INDIVIDUALISM

The great majority of cultures have condemned both individualism and acquisitiveness. They have rejected merit and achievement as formal criteria for ranking individuals, because talent is randomly distributed and likely to violate hierarchical conventions. Wealth has likewise been considered a fallible guide to social worth because it could be acquired by outsiders. The original meaning of the Latin word *pretium* was not "price" or "monetary value," but "personal esteem."

In theory, European societies equated value with production for use, not with abstractions like money. Philosophers, like Aristotle, and theologians, like St. Thomas Aquinas, advocated self-sufficiency and condemned usury because it allowed money to breed money. Preindustrial societies were not receptive to the idea that calculated self-interest should govern all transactions, many of which were expected to serve other ends. Even apologists for the trading world, like Daniel Defoe, recognized the futility of endless accumulation.

The propensity to buy and sell is, however, ubiquitous, if not universal. Even the earliest cultures proved unable to prevent and in practice tolerated a measure of individualism and acquisitiveness. In the early modern period, however, what had been vices became virtues; the burden of original sin was replaced by a belief in the per-fectibility of man and a rationale that sanctioned economic self-aggrandizement. Judgment of behavior was relegated to the realm of private conscience and sin ceased to be a matter of public concern.

The early political economists developed a theory of an auto-matic harmonious market in which selfish individualism could create wealth for all—an intellectual innovation that resolved the inner con-flict between individual and social values. The classical economists ignored social costs and made individual greed respectable by calling it an interest. Because market society was clearly more productive than any alternative, the intelligentsia were willing to commodify the world and accept that some would gain at the expense of others.

Weber thought that rationality was the essence and the end of modern society. Capitalism was not speculative investment, but long-range planning based on calculation rather than impulse. To Weber, the spirit of capitalism only had to appear once and then economic factors took over; it was a collective, not an individual force. Sombart, when he examined the role of the Jews in the development of capitalism, repeated the standard anti-Semitic rhetoric about usury and added the preposterous notion that the Jews succeeded by sublimating their erotic feelings.

In fact, the cult of rationality was much earlier than Weber recognized. Contrary to the beliefs of the early anthropologists, non-Western societies and pastoral economies were conceived and organized in rational terms. The ancient Greeks were pioneers of natural law theory and rational thought; although they never regarded exchange as a dominant institution, they were familiar with the hedonistic calculus and with exchange theory. Without the invention and adoption of Arabic numerals, it would have been impossible to develop sophisticated methods of calculation and analysis. The businessmen of the medieval Italian towns were as rational as their descendants in the Renaissance or the Industrial Revolution.

It is extremely doubtful, however, whether rationality can be equated with capitalism. Rational choice can be defined as ordering alternatives in terms of relative desirability. But rationality is neither a formal technique nor an approach that is uniform across society. Rational conduct is possible without rational motives. Within the market, it is limited by constraints of information about commodities and transaction costs, by the vagueness of expected utility, and by uncertainty and time pressures. Rational choice theory and games theory have made explicit the complexity of optimal decision making in the market. Many choices are collective because individuals cannot guess how they will fare. Modern behavioral theories of the firm assume that capitalist organizations constitute a network of relationships.

Rational choice presumes two guesses: about the consequences of a current action and future preferences should those consequences occur. Economic rationality does not specify when to stop searching for consequences. Even though assets were traded and recorded in abstract forms for convenience from the eighteenth century onward, businessmen usually preferred to deal in concrete and tactile entities that had not been separated from social reality. Investment in the future has always been based more on faith than on calculation.

INNOVATION

The West did not acquire global supremacy through investing capital but by exporting and exploiting men, ideas, and technology. Economic change was driven by the growth of population and its diffusion through global migration and settlement. What distinguished European expansion in the world from previous migrations, like those of the Mongols or the Muslims, was that it was accompanied by a shift in knowledge.

If capitalism had a spirit, it was what Keynes called "animal spirits," the willingness to invest in new, risky undertakings. Capitalism could only be advanced by innovative entrepreneurs whose talents could not be inherited or learned and whose responses to economic opportunity could not be predicted or uniquely determined. The Industrial Revolution in England was in one sense a natural outcome of a free-market economy, whose opportunities attracted entrepreneurs who emerged spontaneously to satisfy demand; each phase of growth had its own set of entrepreneurs.

The market was itself created by autonomous, individual entrepreneurs who raised the capital and allocated resources. The entrepreneur is fundamentally different from the capitalist, who is concerned with return on capital, not with innovation; some marxists have equated capitalists with timid bureaucrats who were more to be pitied than envied. Growth has always depended more on the competitiveness, efficiency, and risk-taking of entrepreneurs than on capitalists, who were often cautious rentiers or corporate functionaries concerned with maintaining, not expanding, the economy. The incentive to maximize profits does not necessarily arise out of ownership.

The development of capitalism is inseparable from the growth of literacy and education. The ability to read and write is essential to extend the market, establish accounting procedures, and urbanize the economy. Oral societies certainly practice logic, but written formulations reduce the importance of subjective constructions and generalize explicit norms. Greater literacy devalues the importance of oral and visual culture and broadens the range of experience and contact. In capitalist societies, where knowledge and skill are recognized as a form of capital, education is formalized; it becomes a training process rather than a means of confirming status.

It is technology that above all divides the modern world from all that came before; the Industrial Revolution can be seen as primarily a technological revolution. Only technological innovation, particularly more effective utilization of new sources of energy, could reduce the cost of production and distribution, provide substitutes for scarce raw materials, raise productivity and output per capita, and solve the problems of Ricardian diminishing returns and Malthusian predictions about the consequences of population growth. Without improvements in transportation and means of communication, no global economy would ever have emerged. Despite time-lags in the rate of innovation between countries, most technology once perfected has been transferred easily and cheaply between cultures.

Technological innovation is distinct from and (from one point of view) shapes scientific advance. Technology is fundamentally a mechanical means of achieving objectives conceived in advance. The instinct for invention has always been present in human society. Improvers have existed ever since the idea of invention was invented, though they have usually functioned within a general structure of knowledge and most often have worked to complete unfinished and refine existing techniques. But in the early modern period, new concepts and more efficacious methods of computation began to transform human behavior and accelerate the potential for change. In Francis Bacon's utopia, the *New Atlantis,* the businessmen ally with the progressive intellectuals to ameliorate the human condition. A more detached, dispassionate scientific attitude appeared in which the universe was viewed as independent of and indifferent to man.

Marxists are unsurprisingly hostile to both technological and demographic determinism because they believe in economic determinism. Several different arguments have been advanced to link science and invention with capitalism. One view downplays technology and the market in favor of the entrepreneur; it argues that investment in applied science only acquires importance when it is translated and diffused through innovation. Schumpeter linked capitalism with mathematics and experimental science, equating the rugged individualism of Galileo with the individualism of the rising capitalist class.

Technology, though in practice irreversible, is a dependent variable driven by the relative costs and availability of raw materials and labor. Inventions can be either demand- or cost-induced, but they will only be implemented when the time period and initiation costs are manageable and when the market offers opportunity for profit. Monopoly prices drive the search for alternatives.

While technology is the most distinctive feature of Western history, its link with capitalism is weak. Major technical changes have been successfully introduced in primitive economies with a limited resource base and tested by trial and error. War has proved a greater stimulant than the market because those who wage war are more concerned to win than to contain costs. Nor can any industry continue to grow at a constant percentage rate, because a constant rate of technological innovation cannot be maintained. Refinements are continuously introduced after a major theoretical breakthrough, but additional knowledge acquired from practical experience does not necessarily improve the theory.

Culture is in fact more important than capitalism. Technology usually marches ahead of human society, which is not always willing to adjust to new ways. Once an idea or invention appears, it cannot be undone, but it can be ignored. Although the impact of new technology is usually experienced as a revolution, most inventions exist long before they are used. A highly developed Japan banned the gun because it was considered a threat to the dominant culture. Advanced cultures are not always the most efficient or the most durable. The pressure of conformity can rigidify scientific knowledge. Changes in environment certainly stimulate new ideas, but much invention is a random succession of acts of insight leading to a cumulative synthesis. Cultural restraints on knowledge and lack of opportunity have always proved greater obstacles to progress than lack of ideas.

A PECUNIARY CULTURE

The linkage between capitalism and the arts is well illustrated by the history of painting in Holland during its cosmopolitan Golden Age. Spurred by technical innovations, which reduced costs, and responding to demand boosted by economic expansion, the output of paintings increased dramatically. Although still organized within a traditional guild structure, artists now produced for the domestic market rather than for individual patrons. Art became a commercial commodity that both promoted and was nurtured by realism and the idea of self. Some artists followed their consciences and expressed disquiet and critical doubts about contemporary social and economic conditions. But many others celebrated Dutch achievements and economic progress; their paintings described in abundant detail the capitalist world that provided a market for their talents.

Conspicuous consumption is found in most cultures, usually in ritualistic behavior associated with rites of passage, such as weddings and coming of age. But real consumerism—the inflation of wants and high levels of spending first recognized by Mandeville—was a late development, though it definitely preceded the Industrial Revolution. Markets were limited and expanded very slowly with little advertising of goods until the eighteenth century. Cultural sanctions, such as sumptuary laws, protected the social hierarchy and regulated display of new status. The elite tried to direct and restrain expenditure by the lower orders and was more concerned with how wealth was used than how it was made.

What is open to debate is whether capitalism (and industrialization) was driven by supply or by demand, by production or by consumption, by voluntary choice or by compulsion. One school of thought has argued that open-ended expectations will always rise beyond supply, that social competition and emulation within and between groups will directly or indirectly sustain demand without danger of satiation. Another school has argued that mass production requires one-dimensional consumers conforming to fashion rather than ranking preferences; consumers are not sovereign, but are manipulated by producers who always have the advantage. Demand is not necessarily self-reinforcing because, as goods increase in availability, their character changes and the pleasure that they yield declines.

The traditional marxist argument that capitalism carries within it the seeds of its own destruction has been given several new twists. Capitalism is alleged to destroy itself by undermining the moral values that had originally brought it to life; self-centered and self-interested individualism combine with ceaseless mobility and self-indulgence to destroy the cooperative basis of society and reduce the level of savings and investment necessary to sustain the economic system. Prosperity is followed by institutional rigidity and by economic and technological stagnation as the pioneers age and their children become lazy or change their priorities and turn their talents to other activities. Change follows a generational cycle—from work to play, from thrift to consumption, from entrepreneur to rentier, from bourgeois to aristocrat.

The eighteenth century freed the West from its past; the nineteenth century freed individuals from each other. Although the concept of individualism may sound human, it is in fact an abstract concept. In classical theory, the rational, profit-maximizing, impersonal optimizer is, moreover, always male; women are usually imagined as selfless and cooperative. Ironically, individual preferences did not acquire social momentum until the economy had grown large enough to make each individual unimportant.

The cult of individualism and the pursuit of self- interest are as much a consequence as a cause of economic growth; prosperity created the desire for individuality. In this as in other aspects of capitalist development, it is impossible to separate cause from effect. Some of the alleged linkages, like that between capitalism and religion, turn out to be largely coincidence. Sombart and Weber's "spirit of capitalism" emerges as more of an attribute than a cause; it describes both an attitude that resulted in capitalist behavior and that behavior itself, which led to a shift in incentives. The process of social and economic change was usually two-way and any causal connection can easily be reversed.

5

IDEOLOGY AND
THE RISE OF CAPITALISM

All models of capitalism, even the most refined, suffer from over-simplification, ambiguity, and inconsistency. They fail to describe either the structure or the process of preindustrial societies; nor do they explain why or how change occurred over time. The term *capitalism* has been given so many meanings that it has lost all meaning. It has symbolic importance but little historical reality or explanatory power. When we try to understand the evolution of the modern world, the idea of capitalism constitutes the problem, not the solution.

Ideas have special properties; they can be discredited or can change their meaning over time, but, unlike physical phenomena, once they exist they cannot be destroyed, no matter how absurd. Even erroneous and opaque ideas become facts in their own right, which can be (re)presented and have real and residual consequences. Theories of change identify, label, and then influence the future course of actual changes in society. It is difficult to challenge a system of ideas, like marxism, without employing its terminology and thereby tacitly recognizing the assumptions of the theory.

61

The interesting question is why so vague and misleading a concept as capitalism was first invented and why it has persisted in current usage for so long. There are two different modes of explanation—intellectual and emotional. On the one hand can be perceived the seductive lure of grand theory; on the other hand, the pressing need to explain the injustices of the world and to express the primordial feeling that capitalist societies exploit and enslave their members. In the final analysis, capitalism is a creature of myth rather than of history.

THE HISTORICAL CONTEXT

Historians have adopted descriptive rather than theoretical models to order and impart meaning to the flow of events over time. Although they often concede that some factors of change are indeterminate, if not random, their traditional chronological approach orders individual facts into significant patterns that cohere and recur. Historians recognize the momentum of events and the pressure of external forces, but they also try to account for individual choice and identify the alternative options that are created by human action. Qualitative changes cannot be predicted. Human history is not predetermined but is conditioned by human will and by the exercise of power. Change occurs continuously, but it can be suppressed or delayed and it proceeds at an uneven pace, often transforming one sector disproportionately without affecting the basic culture. It is not universal or absolute, but particularist and relative.

The main division between historians occurs over speed. The evolutionists believe in gradual and piecemeal change with substantial continuity; the revolutionaries, in sudden and irreversible discontinuities. Evolutionary change (though not biological evolution in the traditional sense, whose time span is too extended) provides a satisfactory explanation for much of human history, but not for occasional discontinuities, especially in conceptual knowledge, when one mind-set replaces another.

There has been no single pattern of capitalist development. Although related in marxist theory to the factors of production and in sociological theory to values and behavioral patterns, capitalism is a vague concept that can be applied to any society that has developed beyond subsistence agriculture into a market economy. It is easier to imagine the precapitalist economy than to find a specific historical example. Capitalism can be defined in terms of the market economy, the growth of financial markets, and consumerism, all of which clearly preceded industrialization. But most of the characteristics attributed to it, including those of modernity, were clearly a consequence of the Industrial Revolution, which, though battered as a concept and stretched chronologically, still has some merit because it was largely driven by new technology and energy sources that transformed the economic basis of society. Ironically, the literature has always focused on the transition from feudalism, not on the transition to industrialization.

The capitalist development model has been applied universally over huge stretches of time, even though the chronology, speed, direction, and extent of development has varied in different parts of the world. The temptation to find in premodern history whatever changes the abstract model predicts has proved irresistible, even in the face of empirical evidence. Economic and social models can be true in form and serve as useful similes, even when they are not true in content or context. But no theory is ever accurate in an absolute sense and inductive research has consistently undermined the validity of general theories of society.

Some theorists, both marxist and nonmarxist, reject empiricism completely and flaunt their contempt for facts. They assume the existence of the capitalist system and then look to the historical record for illustrative friendly examples. It is noteworthy that the most dogmatic and simplistic theorists do not cite archival documents but instead other historians, usually of the same ideological persuasion and selectively and out of context. The primary sources are ignored because they are too diverse, ambiguous, and contradictory for those looking for certainties.

Capitalism has to be studied in a functional context. Cultures are not monolithic and cannot exist in a vacuum. All social systems have rigidities and if they fail to adapt, they perish. But they also develop piecemeal and can continue to function even when some sectors have collapsed. The selective process is imperfect and many obsolete elements survive. The rate and direction of change are determined by many economic, social, and political forces apart from ownership of the means of production.

Capitalist societies have not emerged in a linear progression. Whether at the microscopic level of individual relations or the macroscopic level of global exchange, the history of capitalism has been less a relay race than a game of snakes and ladders. All social systems are potentially unstable because they are composed of individuals whose behavior cannot be completely predicted. In human history, every trend is eventually reversed, every advance stopped, every victor toppled. Although biological metaphors can easily develop into false analogies, capitalist economies do seem to have their own life cycle, falling victim to old age, lack of direction, disagreement over priorities, and incompatible ends.

Capitalism cannot be defined in ways that make its empirical existence demonstrable or valid. Like a gene, it is known by its performance, not by its substantive properties. It cannot serve as a benchmark for operational analysis because it is not quantitative and because its functional mechanism is never described. The minimum amount of capital, for example, which distinguishes a capitalist from a noncapitalist economy, is never stipulated. Whether regarded as an economic system or a system of values, capitalism can at best be only a passive structural model, not an agent of change. It cannot move in any direction—up, down, or sideways. It cannot explain anything, when it contains elements of what has to be explained. Indeed, the concept, because it begs so many questions, is an obstacle to analysis.

THE SEDUCTION OF THEORY

Whether expressed as economic, social, or cultural theory, capitalism is fundamentally an ideological construction. Like theology, it can prompt debates akin to Scholastic arguments about the number of angels who can dance on the head of a pin. To marxists, bourgeois ideology has a material basis in the market economy; Weber has been dismissed as a bourgeois ideologue who dissolved real history in spirit. But in fact, marxism is itself a doctrine of the mind, an intellectual abstraction. The failure of all the historical predictions of marxism have made it a purely academic discourse. Alternative ideologies have produced different versions of the truth, all consistent with their assumptions and objectives and all prone to systemic errors.

The social sciences, founded on the human instinct to observe, collect, measure, classify, objectify, and name, were intended to put an end to ideology. They aspired obsessively to generate logical, macro-theories akin to theories in the natural sciences with the analytical power to predict and control human actions. They sought to build a theoretically based, value-free understanding of the underlying external regularities and invisible processes that generate observed behavior. They were interested in final, not in efficient, causes; in pursuit of a moving human target, they anticipated the trajectory of social evolution.

Social scientists might long for, but they cannot emulate the certainties of the natural sciences. Natural scientists, of course, have difficulty escaping from the assumptions and biases of the mental systems in which they have been trained. They can be blind to new evidence or read it incorrectly or dismiss it until it cannot be ignored. Despite the dethronement of Newtonian physics and the introduction of the principles of uncertainty, indeterminacy, and randomness, science can still, however, explain phenomena at least at the level of secondary causes. Anything that functions without human intervention can be reduced to principles and predictions that, if not universal, apply in a high percentage of cases with a high degree of probability. Theories must withstand repeated experimental testing.

But the human sciences, including economics, deal with humans and infinite variables. Patterns of behavior can be discerned, but because they are not universal, they cannot serve as laws. As the new historicists have pointed out ad nauseam, positivists and social scientists have never succeeded in attaining objective knowledge of social reality. Their grand theories have been based on subjective assessment and a biased methodology. It has been falsely assumed a priori that human nature is constant. The evidence of empirical facts that are independent of a theoretical framework has been rejected, thereby reducing human history to philosophy teaching by examples.

The popularity of an abstraction, such as capitalism, derives from a fondness for model building and for rationalizing from general propositions. Model builders abhor exogenous factors and doubt. It is true that phenomena have to be distinguished before their relationship can be explained, that categorization is the basis of most intellectual thought. But the insistent appeal of connective systems, which reduce the world to order, reflects deep emotions. Intellectuals seek for total answers; they fear the irrational, the chaotic, and the inexplicable. They refuse to accept the random and the accidental in history and they prefer to believe that culture is immutable. They need a cognitive and moral map of the universe in order to assert human authority. They expect certainty and assurance—whether perfection in the present or a utopia in the future. They are drawn to blanket explanations and to single causes in their search for the prime mover, the motor of change. The philosophical rebellion against the universalism of the enlightenment has had little impact on the status of political economy.

For those deterred by the technical complexities of the new economic history, the idea of capitalism provides a comprehensive account of how change is promoted, stabilized, and sanctified. It offers an all-embracing explanatory system that reduces the incoherence of human history to an intelligible, orderly progression of events with dramatic watersheds. A simple thesis with few qualifications can be argued with greater force and is easier to understand and to propagate. Capitalism is a convenient short-hand expression that provides a snappy title and a framework for writing. It is much easier to construct a book around a model with familiar parameters and a captive audience. Stagnant disciplines have been able to postpone extinction by spicing up their standard fare with the fashionable sauce of capitalist interpretation.

It is important to recognize, however, that what purports to be an explanatory structure is in fact a belief system, in which individuals can indulge the fantasy of final causes. They are seduced by the notion of one absolute, one simple explanation for everything; once converted and committed to an exclusive goal, they feel no need to stoop to collect facts, because they already know the truth. Intellectual laziness and cowardice breed ignorance, complacency, and conformity.

Unlike a scientist, the theorists of capitalism are not looking to be proved wrong. Once the initial premise is accepted, any challenge can be explained away in terms of the system by deduction from overriding principles. Theories of capitalism can be as rarefied and metaphysical as any religion. Marxist apologists are really the last of the Schoolmen, if there is likely ever to be a last Schoolman. The true believer has no reason to keep an open mind and seeks only for confirmation. He is content to retreat from reality and concentrate on harmonizing inconsistencies in his belief system.

Reputations have frequently been built on calculated flights of imagination, on the willingness to generalize speculatively from the evidence, to draw conclusions that seem to be important and relevant, even if they are also wrong. The most acclaimed historians have been those who have been able to condense the historical record into a brief and coherent narrative. Unfortunately, abbreviation leads to distortion. The past can only be reconstructed by taking a small slice, but there is no foolproof way in which this slice can then be related to the whole. Historians of capitalism are only able to generalize about huge periods of time because they have a predetermined view of the world and because they are interested in representing, not in documenting, reality. Inevitably, the categories take over and become divorced from what they purport to describe. Truth becomes simply whatever the model predicts. In the quest for a meaningful universe, the complexity of human history is reduced to binary categories. Change is categorized as the victory of one culture or stage of culture over its polar opposite, either directly or indirectly through a dialectical process. In fact, history is a mess; the events of the past never fit neatly into a perfect model. No theory allows anyone to deduce the facts; models do not test, but simulate, historical reality. The idea that society moves as a totality is a holistic confusion.

A CONVENIENT SCAPEGOAT

The idea of capitalism did not exist before the Industrial Revolution and it acquired currency as the essential Manichean bogeyman of socialist theory. It was a retrospective invention by intellectuals (primarily, but not exclusively, marxists) who hated modern, technology-driven, industrial society and who wished to predict its destruction. The Institutional economists denounced what they considered an obsession with the market economy as a capitalist conspiracy fomented by big business corporations and by technology. Although closely linked by its detractors with colonialism, capitalism was nonetheless a Eurocentric concept that could only have emerged in the society that it alternately justified, explained, and accused.

The ideology of capitalism is fundamentally an ideology of discontent based on personal belief rather than social consciousness. Hostility to capitalism was fueled by egalitarianism and by frustration at the injustices of life, by a sense of loss of community and dignity, and by the deep-rooted feeling that economic growth was achieved at the expense of the masses. Even those who have recognized the benefits of capitalism have been disappointed that its full potential has never been realized.

Why, it was asked, is the world not what it might have been? The social reformers adopted a normative methodology, reading their ideal society back into the past and displaying a greater interest in the distribution than in the creation of wealth. In one respect Marx was trying to reconstitute a world in which the whole economic process was controlled by the community, in which society was the family writ large. Those who wished to put the clock back forgot that it was the market and a contractual society that had fostered humanitarian values, that communal societies and their value systems are repressive. As N. S. B. Gras put it, the precapitalist age was not a golden age in which man walked with God. Agrarian societies are stratified and inegalitarian with coercive deference. The alleged wholeness of life in precapitalist society and the mutuality and solidarity of the "traditional" family are both inventions. The fundamental conflict between individual choice in the market and socially and ethically determined needs has made current theories of market socialism somewhat implausible.

The enemies of entrepreneurial and rentier capitalism were driven by moral repugnance and distrust of the profit-maximization of economic man and by aesthetic and spiritual unease with commercialization. Their approach was qualitative, not quantitative and utilitarian; they feared the loss of humanity itself. Man, not money, they believed, should be the measure of all things. Others reacted against the machine and its products, which had replaced creative human labor. They adopted as their ideal an agrarian society in which consumption was limited by supply. Consumerism was denounced (often hysterically) for aggravating inequality, for polluting human sensibility, and for subordinating or destroying weaker, but morally superior, cultures. The more successful the new economic order, the louder the opposition.

Schumpeter, in his pessimistic later years, came to believe that capitalism would be destroyed by its own success, that it created an inimical social and political climate. Entrepreneurship, he thought, would be undermined by bureaucrats, who tolerated but never appreciated innovation. The young and the idealistic would vent their emotional and intellectual dissatisfaction and attack the economic foundations of the capitalist culture. The political traumas of youth would eventually become the ruling academic ideology, since scholarship had little connection with reality.

It is true that a majority of both intellectuals and bureaucrats on the right as well as the left have been no friends of capitalism. Although it was industrialization that largely created and funded an intelligentsia of professionals, they chose to vigorously oppose money making, particularly in the private sector. This was partly the result of a guilty conscience, because they were the prime beneficiaries of the new economic order. One of the many ironies of capitalist culture is that the anticapitalists are often financed by educational institutions and charitable foundations endowed by capitalists. It was partly because capitalism provided a scapegoat on which all the insoluble ills of the world, such as war, irreligion, philistinism, and poverty, could be blamed. To imagine Western high culture without capitalism to attack is to imagine the novel without adultery.

It was partly pique; the intellectuals felt that their status and talents were not properly recognized. The market value of intellectual output is in fact far below factor input. The goals of intellectuals in a market economy are likely to be ignored, because they are not shared by the masses, whereas they have more power and importance in a planned economy. In the eyes of the intelligentsia, the market was too egalitarian and threatened both moral freedom and professional virtues. In fact, the service norms of the professions were careerist, monopolistic, and self-serving, virtually indistinguishable from the alleged value system of capitalism.

In one sense, too, the idea of capitalism was a product of romantic longing for a utopian alternative to industrialization, urbanization, and the alienation of the workforce from any real purpose. Now that the artisan has been virtually eliminated, for example, his past has been idealized by postindustrial moderns. Successive generations of bohemians have denounced the boredom and lack of passion of the bourgeoisie. Paradoxically, as marxism has lost its political credibility and appeal in the real world, its historical sociology has been widely embraced as an explanatory system among intellectuals always prone to seduction by lost causes. As Seneca once said, innocence comes from ignorance.

THE POWER OF MYTH

No one would dispute the convenience of abstract archetypes or deny that they can be useful tools when ordering and reconstructing events. The "rise of capitalism" does serve a limited purpose as a short-hand expression for the real changes in wealth, organization, and scale of economic activity that took place in early modern Europe. Historians shape historical facts for their readers and make them comprehensible by selection. The past is created, not found; it can only be interpreted through the eyes and prejudices of the present. To paraphrase Heisenberg, what we observe is not history but the past exposed to our method of questioning.

The idea of capitalism has, however, been borrowed, often by those who lack any knowledge or understanding of economic history or economic principles, to try to explain all facets of preindustrial society—social change, shifts in political power, the role of bureaucracy, empire building and recurrent warfare, legal innovations, religious dissidence, enthusiasm and secularization, gender relations, the restructuring of the family, innovations in science and technology, the evolution of new literary forms, and the expansion of the fine arts.

To explain the whole of human history by reference to capitalism is no different or more convincing than evoking Providence or the Oedipus complex as the magic wand. Through manipulation and abuse, the idea has acquired a life of its own. But capitalism has neither a destiny nor a personal identity. The disciples of Leopold von Ranke succeeded in taking the theology out of history only to have it creep back in the form of the great secular religions.

Concepts do not constitute evidence or explanations or "real forces"; they are tools that compress bulky empirical data. Nor is any factor completely autonomous; in real life there are no independent variables and cause and effect cannot be separated. Capital formation, for example, is both a cause and a result of capitalism. Although what actually happened looks inevitable in hindsight, in fact there are an infinite number of alternative scenarios. To designate the flow of history in one direction is tempting, but mistaken. Despite efforts by historians to construct tidy patterns from events, to identify distinctiveness rather than just differences, the past really has been one damned event after another. Even the emphasis on explaining change may be misdirected, since, in the absence of constraints, change is the normal state and the interesting question is why it does not occur when it might be expected.

It is pointless, though understandable, to yearn for what has been lost. The past can be imitated but never restored, partly because it is already a matter of record. But consciousness of the past provides the perspective necessary to appreciate what is worth keeping in the present. It gives each generation a sense of tradition and a place in time. Some have doubted the authenticity of historical accounts and, if there are impenetrable barriers that make it impossible for a modern sensibility to understand past cultures, then nobody would have a history. But an intelligent reading of the sources brings to light the same problems, the same mistakes, the same human strengths and failings—an exponential growth of knowledge without a corresponding increase in wisdom.

All societies prefer myths to the truth. Historical events transcend reality to become myths and then revert to events. History has always been used for propaganda and for reinforcing myths and justifying or attacking political and economic and religious systems. But knowledge is not advanced by generating fantasies, no matter how entertaining. There is a past that can be understood in its own terms, even if historians gravitate toward what is fashionable, important, or much discussed in their own day. Reinterpreting the past has to be continuous, but if historians are trapped in a theoretical or ideological swamp and if the bedrock of facts is not secure, they have not advanced any further than their predecessors in the eighteenth century.

BIBLIOGRAPHICAL ESSAY

The best brief introduction to the idea of capitalism by a historian is Ronald Max Hartwell, "The Origins of Capitalism," in *Philosophical and Economic Foundations of Capitalism*, Svetozar Pejovich, ed. (Lexington, Mass.: Lexington Books, 1983), pp. 11–23, supplemented by several contributors to *Capitalism and the Historians*, Frederick August von Hayek, ed. (Chicago: University of Chicago Press, 1954). The special case of America is reviewed by Robert E. Mutch, "Colonial America and the Debate about the Transition to Capitalism," *Theory and Society* 9 (1980): 847–863. The early history of the term is discussed by the eminent medievalist Frederic Chapin Lane, "The Meaning of Capitalism," *Journal Economic History* 29 (1969): 5–13.

Many of the best-known studies of capitalism are in effect potted histories of the world constructed around a metatheory. They include numerous works by the German historian Werner Sombart, selections from whose principal work have been translated and published as *The Quintessence of Capitalism*, translated and edited by M. Epstein (New York: M. Fertig, 1967). France is represented by the historical geographer Fernand Braudel, *Afterthoughts on Material Civilization*, translated by Patricia M. Ranum (Baltimore: Johns Hopkins University Press, 1977), and *Civilisation and Capitalism: 15th to 18th Century*, translated by S. Reynolds (Berkeley: University of California Press, 1992), 3 vols. The North American candidate is the radical sociologist

Immanuel Maurice Wallerstein, *The Capitalist World Economy* (New York: Cambridge University Press, 1979); *The Modern World System* (New York: Academic Press, 1974, 1989), 2 vols.; and *Historical Capitalism* (London: Verso, 1983).

Although these authors acquired in their lifetime temporary guru status, none of their works are reliable as histories and they now have mainly antiquarian interest as tracts for their times. A more prosaic, but now dated, narrative approach was taken by Henri Eugene Sée, *Modern Capitalism, Its Origins and Evolution*, translated by Homer B. Vanderblue and Georges F. Doriot (New York: B. Franklin, 1968), and by Norman Scott Brian Gras, *Business and Capitalism* (New York: A. M. Kelley, 1971).

There are numerous recent general surveys of change in the early modern period, including John Greville Agard Pocock, "Early Modern Capitalism" in *Feudalism, Capitalism and Beyond*, Eugene Kamenka and R. S. Neale, eds. (New York: St. Martin's Press, 1975); Theodore K. Rabb, "The Expansion of Europe and the Spirit of Capitalism," *Historical Journal* 17 (1974): 675–689; Robert J. Holton, *The Transition from Feudalism to Capitalism* (New York: St. Martin's Press, 1985); and Robert S. Duplessis, *Transition to Capitalism in Early Modern Europe* (Cambridge: Cambridge University Press, 1997).

An economist's overview is provided by Robert L. Heilbroner, *The Nature and Logic of Capitalism* (New York: Norton, 1985). A monistic interpretation of world history by a neoclassical economist is Douglas Cecil North, *The Rise of the Western World* (Cambridge: Cambridge University Press, 1973). Some perceptive insights are also offered by the historian of technology David S. Landes, "What Room for Accident in History," *Economic History Review* 47 (1994): 637–656.

Two intellectual traditions, which still have their followers, derive from the philosopher Karl Marx and the sociologist Max Weber. Weber is famous for *The Protestant Ethic and the Spirit of Capitalism*, translated by Talcott Parsons, revised by R. Collins (Los Angeles: Roxbury Publications, 1998), which should, however, be contrasted with his mature *General Economic History*, translated by Frank H. Knight (1927; reprinted New Brunswick: Transaction Books, 1981). Among the better commentaries on Weber are Randall Collins, *Weberian Sociological Theory* (Cambridge: Cambridge University Press, 1986), and Robert J. Holton and Bryan S. Turner, *Max Weber on Economy and Society* (New York: Routledge, 1989). See also Hartman Lehmann, "The Rise of Capitalism," in *Weber's Protestant Ethic*, H. Lehmann and Guenther Roth, eds. (Cambridge: Cambridge University Press, 1993), pp. 195–208, and Gordon Marshall, *In Search of the Spirit of Capitalism* (New York: Columbia University Press, 1982).

Some useful preliminary guides to the marxist historiography of capitalism are Maurice Herbert Dobb, *Studies in the Development of Capitalism* (New York: International Publishers, 1964); Harvey J. Kaye, *The British Marxist Historians* (New York: St. Martin's Press, 1995); Alastair MacLachlan, *The Rise and Fall of Revolutionary England* (New York: St. Martin's Press, 1996); Ellen Meiksins Wood, *The Pristine Culture of Capitalism* (New York: Verso, 1991). Two brilliant commentaries on capitalism in the marxist tradition, now available in English, are Rudolph Hilferding, *Finance Capital*, Tom Bottomore, ed., translated by Morris Watnick and Sam Gordon (Boston: Routledge and Kegan Paul, 1981) and Georg Simmel, *The Philosophy of Money*, D. Frisby, ed., translated by Tom Bottomore and D. Frisby, 2d edition, enlarged (New York: Routledge, 1990).

The stages by which capitalism developed have attracted many different responses ever since the famous article of the Belgian historian Henri Pirenne, "The Stages in the Social History of Capitalism," reprinted in *Class, Status and Power*, Reinard Bendix and Seymour Martin Lipset, eds., 2d edition (New York: Free Press, 1966), pp. 97–107. A survey of the debate over agrarian capitalism is provided by R. Allbritton, "Did Agrarian Capitalism Exist?" *Journal Peasant Studies* 20 (1992–1993): 419–444. Mercantile capitalism is discussed by Patrick O'Brien, "European Economic Development," *Economic History Review*, 2d ser. 35 (1982): 1–18. The debate on the connection between capitalism and slavery is surveyed in *Capitalism and Slavery Fifty Years Later*, H. Cateau and S. H. H. Carrington, eds. (New York: Peter Lang, 1999). The links between capitalism and the Industrial Revolution are explored in *Failed Transitions to Modern Industrial Society*, Frederick Krantz and Paul M. Hohenberg, eds. (Montreal: International Center for European Studies, 1975), and Donald Cuthbert Coleman, *Myth, History and the Industrial Revolution* (Rio Grande, Oh.: Hambledon Press, 1992).

The orthodox view of markets, as outlined by Israel M. Kirzner, *The Meaning of Market Process* (New York: Routledge, 1992), has been challenged by Karl Polanyi, *The Great Transformation* (Boston: Beacon Press, 1985), and by Karl Gunner Persson, *Pre Industrial Economic Growth* (Oxford: Blackwell, 1988). In contrast, the precocity of markets has been argued by M. Bailey, "The Commercialization of the English Economy 1086–1500," *Journal of Medieval History* 24 (1998): 297–311, and by several contributors to *The Market in History*, Bruce Louis Anderson and A. J. H. Latham, eds. (London: Croom Helm, 1986). The intellectual debate over the ethics of capitalism in the early modern period is neatly dissected by Albert O. Hirschman, *Rival Views of Market Society* (Cambridge, Mass.: Harvard University Press, 1992).

The classic economic theory of entrepreneurship is Joseph Alois Schumpeter, *The Theory of Economic Development*, translated by R. Opie (1934; reprinted New Brunswick, N.J.: Transaction Books, 1983). A useful starting point in the vast literature on the history of individualism is Alan MacFarlane, *The Culture of Capitalism* (Oxford: Blackwell, 1987), and Joyce Oldham Appleby, *Capitalism and a New Social Order* (New York: New York University Press, 1984). On other connections between individualism and capitalism, see R. Cotterell, "The Development of Capitalism and Contract Law," in *Law State and Society*, ii, Bob Fryer et al., eds. (London: Croom Helm, 1981), pp. 54–69; N. Folbre and H. Hartman, "The Rhetoric of Self Interest," in *The Consequences of Economic Rhetoric*, Arjo Klamer, Donald N.

McCloskey, and Robert M. Solow, eds. (Cambridge: Cambridge University Press, 1988), pp. 184–203; Paddy Ireland, "Capitalism without the Capitalist," *Journal Legal History* 17 (1996): 41–73.

Theories of capitalism have been applied to histories of women and the family and to gender theory by Roberta Hamilton, *The Liberation of Women: A Study of Patriarchy and Capitalism* (Boston: George Allen and Unwin, 1978); Margaret George, *Women in the First Capitalist Society* (Urbana: University of Illinois Press, 1988); Carole Pateman, *The Sexual Contract* (Stanford: Stanford University Press, 1988); Constance Jordan, *Renaissance Feminism* (Ithaca: Cornell University Press, 1990); Sylvia Walby, *Theorizing Patriarchy* (Oxford: Basil Blackwell, 1991).

A typical example of the school of criticism that analyzes literary productions in terms of market exchange is Douglas Bruster, *Drama and the Market in the Age of Shakespeare* (Cambridge: Cambridge University Press, 1992). L. Haskell, "Professionalism versus Capitalism," in *The Authority of Experts*, T. L. Haskell, ed. (Bloomington: Indiana University Press, 1984), probes the conflict between bureaucracy and capitalism. The birth of consumerism is analyzed by several contributors to *Consumption and the World of Goods*, John Brewer and Roy Porter, eds. (New York: Routledge, 1993).

The most famous exponent of the view, initially espoused by Marx, that capitalism has inherent contradictions is Joseph Alois Schumpeter, whose arguments are to be found in his *Capitalism, Socialism and Democracy* (reprinted Boston: Unwin Paperbacks, 1987); *The Economics and Sociology of Capitalism*, Richard Swedberg, ed. (Princeton: Princeton University Press, 1991). See also S. Haberle, "Schumpeter's Capitalism," in *Schumpeter's Vision*, Arnold Heertje, ed. (Eastbourne, Sussex: Praeger, 1981), pp. 69–93; Tom B. Bottomore, *Between Marginalism and Marxism: The Economics and Sociology of J. A. Schumpeter* (New York: St. Martin's Press, 1992). A variation on the same theme is Daniel Bell, *The Cultural Contradictions of Capitalism* (New York: Basic Books, 1996). The inherent instability of capitalist economies over time is well illustrated by Charles Poor Kindleberger, *World Economic Primacy 1500 to 1990* (New York: Oxford University Press, 1996).

The reader who tires of the smoke and mirrors of overblown theories should turn to the rich variety of empirical studies produced by traditional economic and social historians who have based their analyses on archival sources. One guide through this literature and the substantive issues is Richard Grassby, *The Business Community of Seventeenth Century England* (Cambridge: Cambridge University Press, 1995).

INDEX

ABOUT THE AUTHOR

Former Oxford historian, Woodrow Wilson International Center Fellow, and current member at the Institute for Advanced Study, Richard Grassby has written several books on social, economic, and art history, including *The English Gentleman in Trade* (Oxford, 1994) and *The Business Community of Seventeenth Century England* (Cambridge, 1995). His most recent study, *Kinship and Capitalism: Marriage, Family and Business in the English-Speaking World 1580–1720,* will be published by the Woodrow Wilson Center Press.